WAYNE
ROONEY

World Cup Heroes

WAYNE ROONEY

Mike Parry

JB

JOHN BLAKE

Published by John Blake Publishing Ltd,
3 Bramber Court, 2 Bramber Road,
London W14 9PB, England

www.johnblakepublishing.co.uk

This edition published in paperback in 2010

ISBN: 978 1 84358 171 0

British Library Cataloguing-in-Publication Data:

A catalogue record for this book is available from the British Library.

Design by www.envydesign.co.uk

Printed in Great Britain by CPI Bookmarque, Croydon CR0 4TD

1 3 5 7 9 10 8 6 4 2

Papers used by John Blake Publishing are natural, recyclable products made
from wood grown in sustainable forests. The manufacturing processes
conform to the environmental regulations of the country of origin.

1

Wayne Rooney was born to be a footballer. He has never considered doing anything else.

'I'm going to play for Everton,' he said when, as an eight-year-old, he was asked by a teacher what he was going to do when he left school.

'But what will you do if that doesn't work out?' the teacher enquired.

Being unusually positive for a boy of his years, he replied, 'It *will* work out. I am going to play for Everton.'

Anybody who had ever seen the youngster from Croxteth kick a ball knew by instinct that this was no idle boast. Train driver Bob Pendleton was a talent scout for his beloved Everton in his spare time. Bob was a man who could spot raw talent a mile off. He'd watched hundreds of matches in his lifetime, most of them unmemorable, and it had been a long time since he had seen a lad with the kind of gift that could make his hairs stand on end. He was beginning to wonder if he'd ever experience the spine-tingling thrill of witnessing a new star in the making.

Rooney was just nine years old, playing for

Copplehouse Under-10s in the Walton and Kirkdale Junior Football League, but destiny was standing on the sidelines huddled in an anorak, and the boy's life was about to change forever.

Proud Bob recalls, 'You could tell he was special straight away. When you see someone special, you just know, you feel your hair rising.'

It was a feeling only too familiar to the managers of the tiny Copplehouse Colts team, retired window cleaner Nev Davies and delivery driver John McKeown. They had taken a call from the pub team at the Western Approaches in 1994, who explained they were an Under-12 side, but that they had a boy playing for them who was just nine years old and who was a scoring sensation. Would they like to take a look? Would they! The duo shot over to the Rooney home in Croxteth the next evening.

'We headed over to the Rooney place and Wayne was outside, kicking a ball around in the street,' McKeown recalls. 'We spoke to his mum and arranged to take a look at him the next day. Well, we had become quite blasé about meeting parents, giving trials and saying yes or no to young kids. This time we saw Wayne unleash a stunning overhead kick; he looked years ahead of anyone we had ever seen and we literally drove at 70mph back to his house to complete the signing. He was phenomenal. All he ever wanted to do was score and he was miles better than anyone else.'

And Nev, whose son Ryan used to set up young Rooney's goals from midfield, remembers predicting the fledgling star's rise to greatness. He said, 'From the off, I said he would be better than Michael Owen or Robbie Fowler. He always had big, strong thighs and was more in the Alan Shearer mould, riding the tackles and playing with a fantastic awareness. Wayne was unbelievable... always playing in the team a year above. We had him for 18 months. Needless to say, he scored on his debut and once hit 12 in a 14-goal onslaught.

'In the first season he helped us to an Under-10s cup triumph and then we joined Liverpool's top league, the Walton and Kirkdale. He was fantastic there, too. He was so good he never practised with us. He was a throwback to when lads learned their craft in the street. But we picked him up in the minibus on Saturday morning, he'd listen to our instructions and off he would go.

'He was a shy lad, but very attentive. His dad, very often with his mum, was always there encouraging him. He never got on Wayne's back.

'After 40 or so goals in the second season, John and I turned down the chance of a bet: that Wayne would become the youngest kid to play for Everton and then the youngest kid to play for England. Joe Royle pipped him to the Everton part, but after eclipsing Michael Owen as the Premiership's youngest scorer, the England bit – also held by Owen – was too good to miss!'

It was Nev who had tipped off scout Bob Pendleton about the boy. Now, Bob stood rooted to the spot, transfixed by the scene that was unfolding before his eyes. It was a once-in-a-lifetime moment, a moment of unadulterated magic.

'From the word go, the things Wayne could do with the ball, the goals he could score, you could tell he was a natural. Even then, he was so comfortable on the ball, he was just one of those born players... amazing.'

Buzzing with excitement, Bob hastily sought out team manager John McKeown. 'I approached their manager John and asked him, "What's the name of the little fellow?" He looked at me and groaned. "Oh, Bobby," he said. "We've only just signed him. Leave him alone." I stared at him and said, "Leave him alone? You must be joking!"'

'Wayne was strong, dedicated and couldn't stop scoring goals. The manager pointed out his mum and dad – big Wayne and Jeanette – over on the other side of the pitch. I went over and introduced myself and said that I'd like to take the young man into Bellefield for a trial at the Everton Academy. The look on their faces, because they were Evertonians, said it all. I knew I was on to a winner.'

The trouble was that arch-rivals Liverpool had got there first. The club's scouts had seen him performing in a Saturday league in the Bootle area and young Rooney had already been for a training session.

As Nev explains, 'A Liverpool scout had approached me and suggested Wayne have a trial. The Rooneys have always been true Blue, but they agreed I should take him along to Melwood because I was a Liverpool fan. It was strange: he played well and scored several times in a seven-a-side game, but the coaches were standoffish and didn't make a fuss of him.

'Wayne wasn't too disappointed. Next, I told Bob about him. He came to see him and his eyes immediately lit up. This time John, because he supports Everton, went with Wayne and his mum to the Everton Academy, where his performance was noted straight away. It was the end of the 1995/96 season and Wayne never played for Copplehouse again.'

Bob takes up the story. 'Wayne had been for a training

session with Liverpool, but he only ever wanted to do one thing and that was to play for Everton. It wouldn't have mattered what Liverpool said to him, he wouldn't have gone there. His dad, Wayne Sr, also said he wasn't going anywhere else. He was also adamant that he wasn't going to end up with Liverpool.

'I've been asked if I think I'll ever find another Rooney and the answer is always the same – "Jesus, no!" A good friend said to me, "You only find one of them in your lifetime, so sit back and enjoy the ride Wayne is going to give you." And I am enjoying it. It's emotional at times, but I'm sure Wayne's going through the same!'

Lifelong Everton fan Rob 'Macca' McCarthy also remembers the first time he saw young Rooney and began to see for himself that the rumours about a new wonder kid could actually be true.

'I went down to Croxteth one Sunday to watch him playing for a pub team. It was the Western Approaches (The Wezzy) and other players in the team were all in their mid-twenties and looked the sort that loved a good punch-up. Most of them had flattened noses and close-cropped hair. The opposition team were from Speke in south Liverpool and they, too, looked just like the broken-nose brigade.

'When I first set eyes on Wayne, I thought he was going to get eaten alive by the opposition players, who would not have looked out of place as club doormen. But my fears were unfounded and I couldn't believe what I was seeing as Wayne left his prey for dead. As he raced forward with the ball, several of the opposing players would try to kick lumps out of him, but he danced and weaved his way though them.

'I honestly thought that he was going to get hurt by these men, but he gave as good as he got. I heard a couple of the opposing players squeal and groan as they went down under one of Wayne's bone-crunching tackles.

'This was a schoolboy playing, and holding his own, against grown men who liked nothing better than intimidating and giving their opponents harsh tackles. Well, it was they who received a lesson, because nothing that they could do had any effect on young Wayne. He was not in the slightest bit afraid of them. He was fearless.

'I went to watch him on a number of occasions after that. He had the aggression of Graeme Souness and the skills of Diego Maradona and Kenny Dalglish all rolled into one.

'The touchline would be jam-packed with people who had come just to see Wayne play; even arthritic pensioners who would sit there in wheelchairs with their check blankets over their laps. It was probably the only time they would bother to venture outdoors in the week – and this was in the dead of winter.

'These same pensioners were comparing him to the great Duncan Edwards, one of the Busby Babes who perished in the Munich air disaster in 1958: these comparisons were being made by old men who had actually seen Duncan Edwards play. They would also compare him to Billy Liddle, a Liverpool footballing legend from many years ago and they were making these comparisons about a lad who was still in school. He was simply phenomenal.'

Everton's Academy director Ray Hall has worked on the club's youth development scheme for 12 years and has coaxed and cajoled a galaxy of future stars through their paces. But even he was gripped by an instant thrill when he first witnessed Rooney in action. He signed the boy after just one training session.

'I didn't even need that as proof. When you get an experienced scout sitting there quivering while you're talking to the lad, you know he's a special talent,' he told the *Guardian*.

'We had started hearing a lot about this lad, even when he was an Under-9 player. When Bob Pendleton brought him in, he was trembling and he was spilling his tea all over the place because he was so excited.'

Ray knew he had a rare talent on his hands, but it wasn't until he took the lad with an Under-11 team to play at Manchester United's training ground that he recognised that his latest signing was sprinkled with magic. Wayne was just ten years old, but he delivered a performance so stunning that it hushed the awed crowd into silence.

Ray recalls, 'It was an eight-a-side match on small pitches with small goals. There were hundreds of people there. All the parents were on one side of the pitch and the coaches were on the other as the match started. Someone played a ball over. The ball was crossed, but it went behind Wayne. Instead of controlling it or trying to head it, he executed a scissor-kick from 10 to 15 yards out and the ball flew straight into the top corner of the net. There was total silence around the ground; you could have heard a pin drop. Out of nowhere, I heard one parent – Wayne's dad, I think – start to clap. Then it became a slow ripple of applause and within a few seconds everyone was clapping him like thunder, even the United parents were applauding. It was unforgettable.'

The boy wonder later went on to score a record-breaking 99 goals for the Academy's Under-10s in one season.

Hall's department is one of the biggest at Everton, because producing their own home-grown talent is crucial for the cash-strapped club. 'In recent years, we have produced four England internationals in Jeffers, Rooney, Michael Ball and Gavin McCann, plus Richard Dunne for the Republic of Ireland,' he says. 'And five of the ten youngest goalscorers in the Premiership came from here: Jeffers and Rooney again, plus Ball, Michael Branch and Danny Cadamarteri.

'Wayne has done brilliantly. Every challenge he has been faced with he has met and raised the bar. Nothing seems to faze him. He has always played over his own age, which is probably why he's so comfortable with the England squad. He's the youngest, but he's used to that. He's no different from the kid at school who is a gifted mathematician and who has been moved up classes to be with kids of his own ability.'

The Everton Academy was truly a family affair for the Rooneys – back in 1998, Wayne and his brothers Graham and John all played for the club's youth teams. 'It was the first time in history that we had three brothers all playing here at the same time, and all of them were talented.'

As with all kids at the Academy, Rooney was taken under the wing of a welfare officer from the moment he was signed up. It's the officer's job to keep an eagle eye on the boys' development, to ensure that they are not under too much pressure and to prevent them from becoming unhealthily obsessed by performance.

Gently, over time, the youngsters are schooled in the

pitfalls of fame: how to behave in a fashion that brings credit to the game and how to handle attention from the public and media.

Hall says, 'There are five bubbles surrounding a player. Every player has to cope with his own rate of technical development, physical growth, physiological progress and mental development. We have technical coaches and fitness coaches and a medical department and sports scientists, but by far the biggest bubble is their social and emotional development.

'At Goodison Park, players are presented with a code of conduct and every year they are reminded that they have a duty to behave well. If we've done anything for Wayne, we've improved his social life and skills. He was a timid boy when he came here, but we give the players life-skills training on how to manage the media and everything else that goes with the glitz.'

The practice pitches used by the Academy were a mile away from De La Salle, the Catholic school where Rooney was a pupil. Yet he was always the first to arrive; he leaped on his BMX bike the second the school bell rang at 3.30pm and pedalled as fast as his legs could carry him to the patchily turfed theatre of his dreams.

There, alone, he re-created his favourite goals: zig-zagging across the pitch and shooting over and over again with a vivid commentary running in his head, until training started at 5pm.

Hall remembers, 'Wayne never missed a session, never gave us a moment's problem and had this terrific, supportive family that let us get on with the job.'

His former PE teacher at De La Salle, Joe Hennighan,

also remembers Rooney's dedication. 'Wayne was not particularly academic – young lads love sport and if you live in this city there is only one sport they are going to play, and that is football. Once Wayne started playing, it was obvious that he was going to go far. He was a really good competitor and was always very able physically.'

The school, based in tough, inner-city Croxteth, has built a reputation as a breeding ground for top-class footballers – Francis Jeffers was also a pupil and Wayne would later go on to partner him in the duo's first appearances in England's full squad in the friendly against Australia: a hearty consolation for De La Salle after losing its best players to the Everton Academy.

Rooney, always a stocky lad, suddenly shot up in size when he was 13; he towered over the other boys in his class. Briefly his football form suffered as his body adapted, but his unerring discipline never wavered. His worried parents would often call the Academy, concerned that their son had not returned home, but more often than not he would be found pounding the treadmill at the gym.

Sometimes, though, as with any boy, Wayne's halo slipped. He would sneak off to the local bookies with a pal to play on the fruit machines – his height made him appear older than his years – or he would stride off to his uncle Richie's boxing gym for a bout of body-building and sparring with his cousin. His fuming mum would always tear him off a strip when he eventually returned home, attempting to look a picture of innocence.

Today, at 5ft 10in, Wayne's an average height for a player, but his wide-shouldered boxer's physique makes him an unstoppable bulldozer on the pitch. That and

Wayne's cleanness of shot have invited comparisons with former England skipper Alan Shearer. And that's music to the ears of Rooney.

As a youngster, he avidly studied his hero until details of the superstar's legendary goal-getting were etched into his memory. He would later take to the street for an action replay, placing himself in the shoes of Shearer.

'He'd be my ideal strike partner,' Wayne told the official Everton website, 'because I used to watch him as a kid and I tried to model myself around him.'

Wayne's star was soon fixed in the firmament at the Everton Academy. At Under-12 level, he played for the Under-13s; at Under-15 he played for the Under-17s and even the Under-19s. By 16, he was playing with the professionals.

One man remembers the 14-year-old Rooney only too well. Walter Smith, then Everton manager, was sitting in his office at the training ground, tackling paperwork, when he chanced to look up. Outside on the pitch, an Under-17 game was in full flow. Suddenly, Smith felt as though he had been struck by a bolt of lightning, as a bulky, shaven-haired lad let rip a bullet-like shot from the halfway line.

'I just took a couple of minutes to have a look at the game going on outside. I saw this kid run a yard into the opposition half and then unleash this magnificent shot. I don't think it went in, but I remember thinking to myself, My God, who is that?

'It was something I had only ever seen Pelé and David Beckham try. Not many would try that, never mind a youngster. When I asked who he was, our youth-team coach Colin Harvey told me and then said, "By the way, boss, he's only 14!" I was amazed.

'We realised we had a youngster who was very special...
Going into the training ground on a Saturday morning
before first-team games at Goodison, I'd watch Wayne
playing against much older boys, scoring goals from every
angle. It was incredible.'

At 16, to his joy, the devoted Toffeeman got his chance
to stuff Liverpool in the first Under-19 Merseyside derby of
the 2001 season.

Hundreds of fans had converged on Everton's training
ground, Bellefield, and those in the red shirts of Liverpool
were smugly anticipating victory with their team sitting on
a 2–1 lead with just 15 minutes to go. Rooney watched
anxiously from the bench, every fibre of his body tense,
fervently hoping that he'd get the chance to help his team
grab victory from the drooling Red jaws of defeat. Then, as
Liverpool got ready to take a corner, Everton brought on
their deadliest weapon from their schoolboy arsenal.

Rooney strolled on to the pitch; a few moments later,
Everton equalised. Then, with just minutes to spare,
Rooney struck a supernova volley from the edge of the
penalty area that exploded into the Liverpool net. It was
the last kick of the game and it instantly wiped out the
smiles on the Reds' faces: result – 3–2 to Everton;
'Roomania' was born.

The dismay of the Liverpool fans hung heavy in the air
and, later that week, the club made a raid for Rooney,
hoping to prise him away from Goodison Park. But the boy
resolutely pledged his future to the Everton Academy. Such
was the club's glee, it triumphantly paraded Rooney in
front of 38,615 fans during the half-time interval of a
Premiership game against Derby County on 15 December.

One reason that Rooney would never have gone anywhere at that time was because of youth-team coach Colin Harvey, who had built up a strong relationship with the youngster over a number of years. Harvey, himself a legend among Evertonians as a championship winner in 1970 and as someone who had managed the club, has admitted he literally rubbed his eyes the first time he saw Rooney. In his bestselling memoirs, *Everton Secrets*, he wrote, 'He's undoubtedly the best young player I've ever seen, the best Everton have produced and he can become one of the greatest English players of all time. Until Wayne came along, the best youngster I'd ever seen was Alan Ball. I later teamed up with Bally at Goodison and he did it all for Everton and England, winning 72 caps, the World Cup and championship medals. He was the best Everton player in my opinion and my experience.

'My earliest memory comes from a Sunday morning in August 1997 when there was a break in the Under-16s game because of an injury. I happened to glance over to where the Under-11s were playing. As I looked, this kid got the ball on the halfway line, went past four opponents and lashed it into the net. That was my first sight of him – he was still a couple of months away from his twelfth birthday. So I left the Under-16s match and went to see more of this lad in the Under-11 team.

'Any thoughts that what I'd seen was merely a freak were soon dispelled. Wayne did remarkable things on a regular basis. He was stronger than the rest of the kids and I did wonder whether he would develop or level out when the others caught up with him physically. I've seen it happen so often. But not with Wayne. He developed and maintained his strength. I just looked at him and thought that, if he carried on like that, he was going to be a world-beater.'

Harvey was also anxious to try to direct Wayne off the pitch as well as on it. He said, 'I used to give him a lift to his home in Croxteth, or to his grandmother's, after we had got back from games. I'd have a little word in his ear and give him bits of advice about whom he was knocking around with. I told him he must continue to work hard at school. Wayne was always very receptive to things like that. He'd listen and take it all on board. He wasn't an introvert, but very much a quiet, self-contained lad. That was until he stepped onto the field, which is, and always has been, his playground. He always knew exactly how good he was. Even as a youngster I'd pay to watch him play and I mean it.

'Wayne has very kindly said in public that I have helped to make him a better player. But I agree with what Bill Shankly once said, that it's not coaches that make players but mothers and fathers and he's got great parents. All coaching can do is bring out skills and help their natural expression, but all that is meaningless unless you have the sort of inborn talent that the boy possesses. Even if Wayne was having a bad game, he would still do three or four things in a match that would take your breath away. He'd do something that would make your heart beat a little bit faster.'

Wayne's career was moving at lightning pace and he would soon be on the verge of the first team. But, before moving forever into a new stratosphere, Rooney had a single aim: to lift the FA Youth Cup with Everton.

The mesmeric striker was rarely halted on his successful mission, ramming home thunderbolt goals in almost every match. Against Manchester City he scored twice in a 4–2 victory. West Bromwich Albion fared no better, falling victim to the dazzling skills of their young opponent as he bobbed and weaved his way past players as if they were mere shadows and rocketed home two riveting goals, lobbing the keeper from 20 yards for his crushing finale.

Nottingham Forest met the same fate in the quarter-finals, with Rooney executing an amazing scissor-kick for the first goal. Later, he set up a goal for defender David Carney, who thumped home the winner in the 2–1 triumph.

But it was the match against Tottenham Hotspur at White Hart Lane that would start the wave of fruitless bids for Rooney's talent. Spurs manager Glenn Hoddle was gob-smacked by the boy's performance – and was dispirited to discover that he wasn't for sale. The reason was obvious: Rooney had already created a 3–1 lead on aggregate for the Everton team when, in the 37th minute, he unleashed a goal so spectacular that all anybody could do was gawp in wonder, including Hoddle.

Everton had been given a free-kick 30 yards from goal and Rooney, never one to miss an opportunity, reckoned he might just fly one into the net. He sent a disappointing shot curling straight into the Spurs wall but, as the ball cascaded down, Rooney appeared like magic to take it on his chest and, before it had a chance to kiss the earth, sent it crashing into the top corner with his left foot.

He went on to score eight during the campaign, one short of the record shared by Liverpool's Michael Owen and Arsenal's Jeremie Aliadiere, and had 25 goals under his belt by the end of the season.

The best, however, was yet to come.

2

To the world at large, Wayne Rooney's adult career started on 19 October 2002. The goal he scored against Arsenal at Goodison Park that day began what has since become the Rooney legend. As commentator Clive Tyldesley screamed over the roar of the Goodison crowd, 'Remember the name – Wayne Rooney...'

It was a shocking day for Arsenal, but a great day for Evertonians and a brilliant day for every England football fan.

Arsène Wenger had hinted that he expected his team to go through the whole season unbeaten, an ambition that, thanks to Rooney, had to be put on hold for another year. Their defeat also ended their 30-game unbeaten run, stretching way back into the previous campaign.

It wasn't just that he scored with 23 seconds of play remaining. It was the manner of the goal: it was an event.

Rooney, loitering in his favourite part of the pitch, just outside the penalty area, plucked the ball out of mid-air like somebody picking an apple off a tree.

No Arsenal defender saw a threat. And who could

blame them? As far as they were concerned, they were being confronted by a raw young kid who had been brought on in the dying embers of the game with the score at 1–1 for a bit of first-team experience. In their eyes, he was probably a bag of nerves and posed no realistic threat to the meanest defence in the country.

The Arsenal defenders backed away to mark the men around the box. This had the effect of opening up a channel for Rooney, who now saw a clear goal-scoring opportunity.

He steadied himself, but, even as he prepared for the shot, the England keeper David Seaman didn't envisage a problem. The kid was almost 30 yards out and the goal was well covered.

A split second later, an object resembling an Exocet missile flew over his head at an unbeatable speed, shaved the underneath of the cross-bar and ricocheted down over the line.

The Arsenal defenders couldn't quite believe what they had seen. Before hauling himself to his feet, Seaman sat on the ground looking sheepish and feeling foolish that he had been beaten. He wasn't to know that he had just been eclipsed by a boy who, within a few years, was going to be one of the world's great footballers and who, just four short months later, would become a fellow England international.

The goal, which became October's Goal of the Month, was scored by an apprentice footballer, five days shy of his 17th birthday. He had beaten Michael Owen's record as the youngest ever scorer in the Premiership by five months.

And in a truly compassionate gesture, particularly for a boy his age, rather than taking his boots home that day and maybe giving them to his parents or keeping them as a souvenir of his wonder goal, he donated them to a specialist children's hospital, a world-renowned institution where his girlfriend Coleen's disabled sister had been receiving treatment. They were auctioned to raise funds.

After the match, Arsenal manager Arsène Wenger was gracious in defeat. He said, 'We have been beaten by a special goal from a special talent.'

Illustrating all the reasons why he is rightly regarded as one of the world's top club coaches, he went on, 'You don't have to be a connoisseur to see that. He has everything you need for a top-class striker. I haven't seen a better striker under the age of 20 since I've been in England. He's a great prospect for English football.'

For Evertonians, it justified all the hope and expectancy that had been building up about Rooney over the past two to three years. They knew that he was very special. Others within the industry with their ears close to the ground were also aware of the extraordinary nature of the boy Rooney.

The previous season, he had scored eight goals in the FA Youth Cup, though even his prodigious talent could not secure the trophy for his club as the Blues were beaten in the two-legged final by Aston Villa.

It is rumoured that, as a result of those performances alone, Manchester United, Real Madrid, Bayern Munich and AC Milan were alerted by their British scouts to the presence kid from Croxteth.

Everton manager David Moyes was having none of it and, as speculation and rumour developed, he made it clear that not even £15 million would be enough to interest the club in parting with their jewel.

Everton were so excited by Rooney's development from a schoolboy to a young man on the cusp of a brilliant senior career that they held his signing ceremony on the pitch at Goodison at half-time in their Premiership game against Derby.

He signed his scholarship contract worth £80 a week plus generous appearance and win bonuses in front of a packed Goodison Park with his mum and dad by his side.

Apart from Rooney's obvious joy, it was also the proudest moment for Wayne Rooney Sr and Jeanette, the heads of an Everton-daft family who, like every other parent on Merseyside, hoped that one day one of their boys would play for the club.

Again, this had all happened before Wayne had played a single game in the first team. Ironically, in light of all the other footballing records he has created, Rooney missed the opportunity to become Everton's youngest-ever debutant.

Walter Smith, Moyes's predecessor at Goodison, had wanted to play him in February of that year, but was prevented from doing so by FA rules protecting players who are still at school.

He left school the following month, but then his involvement with England in the European Under-17 Championships, where he scored five goals, stopped Moyes from picking him in May.

But these events were only postponing the inevitable: let loose in the first team in pre-season friendlies, he scored eight times in nine games, including two hat-tricks. When he finally made his debut in a competitive fixture for the first team, in Everton's opening game of the new season, a home draw with Spurs, Wayne was a fortnight older than

Joe Royle had been when the club record of 16 years and 282 days was set.

His explosion on to the football stage was not just a reward for his skill. In much the same way as Michael Jackson once said that his childhood had been 'stolen' by the fact that he was a chart-topping singer at just 12 years of age, Rooney could have claimed that his own life as a youngster had been almost totally consumed by football.

The difference is that he wanted it that way and would have had it no other.

3

Although football was Wayne's obsession and it occupied his every waking moment, like any teenage lad, he had another important interest: girls. Or, to be more accurate, one girl in particular: Coleen McLoughlin.

Unlike most footballers' relationships, Wayne Rooney's romance with wife Coleen began way back when he was a schoolboy, and those solid foundations are what have sustained the couple through stormy times.

Rooney has been accused of cheating on Coleen and it was rumoured that the incensed Coleen even threw her £25,000 engagement ring into a squirrel sanctuary near their former Formby home. But the trials and tribulations of fame, resulting in their dirty linen being washed in public with the heartbreaking allegations that go with it, have only served to forge a deeper respect and love between the young couple.

'He is the person I love and who I want to stay with for the rest of my life,' she said after the couple had been engaged for two years. 'Friends and family had warned me against dating him. They also tried to persuade me that we were too young to set up home. But I have no regrets, because I will stand by him no matter what. I had no hesitation when Wayne proposed to me.'

The couple's romance also survived claims that Rooney had visited a Liverpool brothel – allegations he initially hotly denied, insisting that he had been the victim of a sting. Then pretty brunette Emily Fountain, 20, claimed that he took her to a private room in a nightclub and kissed her. The computer-sales girl said she snogged Rooney at the trendy Odyssey Bar in Altrincham, Cheshire, as he celebrated victory over Chelsea with a group of his team-mates.

But Coleen told the *Mirror*, 'There are some evil and jealous people out there who clearly want to spoil things between Wayne and I, but there are more important things to think about and they should give it a rest. Nothing will come between us. We'd barely been together a year when he got my name tattooed on his arm.'

It was Wayne who romanced Coleen – and she made him work at it all the way. But, for Wayne, the prize was worth working for.

'She's gorgeous looking, but she's also got a great personality. She's a dead special person and I can't think of anybody who's a patch on her. From the moment I kissed her – I was just 14 – I always knew she was the girl for me and that feeling never changed. It just stayed strong and I enjoy every moment with her.'

The couple's fledgling romance started at school, where the passion that burned in Rooney's soul and set his feet alight had already made him a playground hero. Soccer was his passion but he was also beginning to show an interest in girls.

Already standing head and shoulders above his classmates, Wayne cut an impressive figure on the tough Croxteth council estate that he called home. But he was a bashful lad, quiet and shy. The acne-plagued awkwardness of youth, with limbs and hair sprouting, hormones running wild and emotions sky-high, hadn't passed him by.

But Wayne couldn't afford to be distracted by girls and, anyway, the cocky charm of the skirt-chaser wasn't in his nature. He was already too streetwise, too thoughtful, too self-aware for that, and, what's more, he had been counselled by parents who were only too familiar with the pitfalls of estate living.

Single motherhood was a fact of life on many of the estate's streets and within his own extended family; his dad's favourite pub, The Dog and Gun, on the corner of the road where they lived, had closed down after a police investigation into drug dealing; and petty vandalism was rife.

The potential for brief but potent youthful fumblings that shatter dreams had also been carefully explained to Wayne at the Everton Academy, where a glittering future now lay within his grasp. Avoid temptation and confine conquest to the pitch: a wised-up Wayne understood the value of cautious discipline.

Still, there were girls, those he knew as friends: the sisters of his pals; his cousins; his classmates… but one girl in particular had captivated the wary lad and his affected boyish indifference slowly evaporated as he came to recognise the unsettling feelings she evoked in him.

Although he didn't know it at the time, Rooney was falling in love. And Coleen McLoughlin was the girl who had captured his heart.

Coleen, a pony-tailed, dark-blonde girl with clear, green eyes, was just 12 years old when she first met Rooney. She was a pupil at the strict, all-girls St John Bosco Roman Catholic school where Wayne's mum, Jeanette, worked as a part-time cleaner, and was a friend of Claire, his cousin and the sister of one of the soccer star's favourite cousins, Thomas.

It was Thomas's dad Richie who owned the boxing gym where Wayne and his younger brothers Graham and John would often sit and watch football matches on the widescreen telly with their mates, including Coleen's brothers Anthony and Joe. Eight families from the close-knit Rooney clan were neighbours on the Croxteth estate and their friendships often intertwined.

Coleen says, 'I can remember Wayne playing football in the street with my brothers. We were only 12 when we first met and we were all just mates at first.'

Coleen's parents, Colette, a hospice care worker, and Antony, a labourer, lived a few minutes' walk around the corner from Wayne's family and, like Wayne Sr, her dad had been a keen amateur boxer. He helped Wayne's uncle Richie to run the gym and had coached young Rooney there as a boy. The families shared a strong Roman Catholic faith and a fierce desire to see their children succeed.

Wayne was comfortable around Coleen. She was a no-nonsense girl who, like him, harboured driving ambition. Since the age of six, she had wanted to be an actress and, like him, was hard-working and wholly dedicated to her goal.

Wayne says, 'By the time I was 14, I knew I fancied her. But Coleen wasn't really interested in boys. She was a goody who did her homework. All I was interested in was football.'

The couple's romance grew from its beginnings as a steady, innocent friendship that flourished on the street corners of Croxteth. As the afternoon light began to fade, Wayne would often ride out on his mountain bike to fetch paper-wrapped chips from his local chippie, before returning to find Coleen sitting on a wall, watching as her brothers and their mates played footie. He'd plonk himself down beside her, offering her chips with a nonchalance that belied his beating heart.

Coleen remembers, 'We used to spend hours hanging around on the street corner, just talking to each other. At first we were just mates, but then we began to spend more time together and we became best friends.'

But Wayne was too shy to ask Coleen for a formal date. She was the girl next door he'd known since childhood: an ambitious, bright girl whom he counted as a trusted friend. He was uncertain whether the tender affection he felt towards her was returned and, in a quandary, played the joker to try to gauge her feelings.

'I used to pull little stunts to try and get close to her... I desperately wanted to kiss her, but I didn't know how. I remember once I pretended to have contact lenses that I couldn't get in my eyes and asked her to have a look and see if my eyes were OK.

'I could never get the courage to ask her out properly or kiss her. I used to try and ask, but she wouldn't take it seriously. I invited her out on loads of dates – to the chippie, to the pictures, I even promised to take her to Paris for Valentine's Day if she'd come on a date. She was gorgeous looking and had a great personality, but she always thought I was skitting her.'

It wasn't until Wayne turned knight in shining armour, riding to the rescue after spotting his princess in trouble, that he managed to win his date – and then, only after enlisting the help of Claire, his cousin and Coleen's friend.

'My day came when the chain came off Coleen's bike. She was with my cousin Claire and I saw them trying to fix it. I was on my way home and stopped to help. I used it as an excuse to chat to Coleen, asking if I could borrow her video of *Grease*. I've always been a fan. I loved that movie and knew she did too.

'When Coleen went inside to get the video, I grabbed Claire and asked her to get Coleen to come on a date with me. By then, I was fed up of asking. But this time, Coleen said yes!'

The couple shyly walked across the street, with Wayne's heart thudding as he knew his moment had come: he was going to steal a kiss off the girl he adored. He steered her carefully towards the church, a place that was well known as a local lovers' lane where young sweethearts met for secret snogs.

'We went for a walk; we knew we were going to snog. I took her to the back of the church: it was the first kiss that ever mattered to me; she was special. I knew then that we were made for each other, but I was lost for words. Coleen did most of the talking – I think she was shocked at what a fantastic kisser I was!

'I walked her home and I phoned her as soon as I got in and asked her for a proper date. The next day we planned to go out. I'd arranged to meet my friends in town and I was so excited I bought a whole new outfit – a green jumper, jeans and brown shoes.'

The couple went to The Showcase Cinema, a frayed, old-fashioned picture house a short stroll from their homes to see *Austin Powers: International Man of Mystery*, followed by cheeseburger and chips at a fast-food restaurant close by. It was their first proper, unchaperoned date and Wayne walked her home, a shy acknowledgement between them that, now, they were officially an item.

The coals of the sweethearts' passion were ignited, but their romance was forced to slow burn as Wayne's meteoric rise to stardom took off. He was just 16, earning £90 a week at Everton, when he hung up his school uniform at De La Salle school for the last time at Easter.

Just seven months later, he became a fully fledged member of the Everton elite, signing his first professional contract and becoming one of the richest youngsters in world football, earning up to £18,000 a week, including bonuses.

The three-year-deal – the maximum length for a 17-year-old – made him the highest-paid teenager in Everton's history, earning the kind of mind-boggling money each week that many from his home turf in Croxteth didn't see in a year.

The fuse of superstardom had been lit and the football world was fizzing with excitement as Rooney scored goal after sensational goal for the club's youth team. A £2 million endorsement deal with Nike plopped through the letterbox just weeks later and was signed with a trembling flourish of his pen by the disbelieving lad.

Coleen had celebrated her 16th birthday on 3 April 2002, just a few weeks before Wayne had left De La Salle school, and so certain was he that she'd remain a permanent fixture in his life, he'd had her name tattooed on his right arm.

Her parents were strict about time-keeping, anxious that she should prepare for the exacting A-levels she was due to begin at St John Bosco sixth form in September, and determined that what might be no more than a fleeting teenage infatuation should not distract their clever daughter from her studies. But Wayne already knew that Coleen was the girl for him. 'I'd stopped going out with my mates as much, although I still played football before I saw her every night! I just wanted to be with her.'

As Wayne wandered slowly home, his clockwork mind quietly ticking, he felt a bubble of happiness well inside him and he smiled: he knew that Coleen was the girl he wanted to marry. It was just a matter of time before he'd let her know. It never occurred to him that the whole world would want to know, too.

4

Rooney, instantly promoted to the Toffees' first-team squad, took just weeks to smash his way into Everton's record books. On 24 September, in a bitterly contested match against Wrexham, the teenage powerhouse became Everton's youngest-ever scorer, sent on as a sub to belt home two astonishing goals in the Worthington Cup win.

But it was that spectacular last-minute goal against Arsenal a month later that had left the football world open-mouthed, drooling at the sheer, audacious brilliance of the boy: a boy still five days short of his 17th birthday.

It was a goal that saw world-class keeper David Seaman, the England team's safe pair of hands, left sitting helplessly on his backside: it also saw Rooney become the Premiership's youngest-ever scorer. An awe-inspiring legend was being carved on the hallowed pitches of England's Premiership clubs and, just a few months later, the whole world would hear the story. Knock, knock, England was calling...

Rooney was so staggered to be asked to play for England that he immediately assumed Sven-Goran

Eriksson meant he was up for the Under-21s. But he was wrong. From the very first training session, the rest of the England squad were impressed by his burgeoning power.

'Well, I got the ball, managed to beat a few players and then chip the goalie,' explained Wayne, as if it were the most obvious thing in the world for a kid of his age to be doing against the best footballers in the country. 'It was one of my first sessions and all the players just looked at me and started to clap.'

His debut match against Australia at Upton Park in February 2003 was a humiliating 3–1 defeat for England: an historic victory for the Socceroos that sent English hearts plummeting. But a hero had emerged from the ashes of defeat – Rooney had outperformed some of the nation's biggest football names: his place in the galaxy of soccer's greats was already becoming assured. He started the second half in place of Michael Owen, becoming England's youngest-ever player at the age of 17 years and 111 days, breaking the record that had stood for 123 years from James Prinsep of Preston, who few had previously heard of.

And, just as he had done with his boots after the Arsenal game, he generously donated his first England shirt to children's charity Ronald McDonald Children's Charities, an organisation that helps parents with desperately ill children, for auction. The shirt was framed; it had the details of the game stitched on the front, England vs Australia, 12 February 2003, a big, bold white number 23 and the Three Lions emblem. Across the top of the number is written: 'Best Wishes, Wayne Rooney' – and I was lucky enough to win it!

With the thrill of his record-breaking game still coursing

through his veins, Rooney dashed back to share his first moments of glory with Coleen. He was dropped off at her parents' home by a friend – an England star he may have been, but he still hadn't passed his driving test. Later, as twilight blanketed the ragged Croxteth skyline, he shared a bag of chips, a bottle of cola and a kick-about in the street with his mates: it was just an ordinary evening for the extraordinary boy who had the world at his feet.

It would be the last time he'd need to buy his own Coke – within weeks, Rooney had signed up with Coleen to a £500,000 advertising campaign with the fizzy-drinks giant. It was a team effort, just like Posh and Becks before them.

And, just a month later, the lad who had worn hand-me-down trainers was revelling in the luxurious surrounds of the England training camp at La Manga. It was a million miles from the caravan in a Welsh holiday park near Rhyl where he'd spent childhood holidays with his cousins.

La Manga is a five-star resort, packed with the kind of exotic luxuries that Wayne had only ever seen in the pages of glossy magazines that had been carelessly discarded in the players' lounge at Everton for others to flick through.

It held few mysteries, though. He'd been carefully coached from an early age by the team at Everton's Academy and had then been taken under the wing of Alan Stubbs, a senior club player, who had ensured that the boy from the backstreets was well steeped in the polish that would help him blend in.

And Wayne wanted Coleen with him. The couple's relationship was by now a firm fixture. Wayne had been welcomed into Coleen's family, staying at their home overnight to share tender moments with his girl. 'Coleen had a TV and video in her bedroom and we'd go upstairs together to watch things like *Grease* or *Armageddon*. I remember I told Coleen I loved her first. We were watching *Pearl Harbor*, sitting on the sofa at her house. I just told her I loved her; I think the film was a bit of an emotional one and it just came over me!

'Even when I used to go home, which was just down the road, I'd phone her as soon as I got in the door to tell her I was back. Then I'd text her to tell her that I loved her, and I'd often pick her up from school.'

The rock-solid relationship met with the approval of Coleen's mum and dad. They recognised Wayne's serious intent – and their daughter's love for him – and agreed to allow Coleen to make her first trip alone with Wayne, to La Manga. She had to sit an English exam on the day the squad flew out, but joined her hero a day later. And she was petrified! 'I didn't know what to expect. I was dead scared,' she admits.

She said, 'I rang Wayne and asked him to find out what kind of clothes the women were wearing. I told him to look when they came down for breakfast, but he told me everyone had eaten in their rooms. I was really worried I would take the wrong clothes or not know what to do.'

Realising she couldn't rely on Wayne for fashion advice, before she left, she enlisted her mum for an express shopping trip around the designer stores of Manchester, a short hop from Liverpool and boasting a posh Harvey Nichols, to pick up the glitzy dresses, sunglasses and the trendy red Burberry bikini that would see her elevated to cover-girl status from the minute she touched down on her sun lounger.

She said, 'My mum rang me to tell me there were pictures of me all over the newspapers. I couldn't believe it – I was dead worried what I looked like in my bikini!'

She needn't have worried. The girl Wayne affectionately called 'Babe' looked gorgeously natural – a refreshing change from the sleekly expensive artifice surrounding her – and was soon the tabloids' darling: her natural curves, dewy young skin and innocent charm quickly elbowed Victoria Beckham off the front pages.

At first, naturally, Coleen was overawed by the world-famous celebrities around her. Surreally, people she'd only ever seen in pictures sat beside her at breakfast, chatting with their families about plans for the day over freshly baked croissants, at ease and at home in the plush surroundings: Liverpool striker Michael Owen, his baby daughter Gemma nestled in his arms, lounged in the sun with his partner Louise Bonsall, sharing a joke with Wayne; Steven Gerrard, another hero-worshipped Red, and his stunning girlfriend Alex, soaked up the 80-degree heat near by, teasing the couple with Scouse humour and beginning a bond that would later see him become a pal to Rooney as the lad sweltered under the unwavering glare of the media spotlight.

Queen bee Victoria offered the hand of friendship, inviting Coleen to spend the day with the girls while the boys sloped off for a game of golf – a first for Wayne but, inevitably, not a last – or to challenge each other at go-karting.

Coleen was soon gossiping away with the rest of them, relaxed in a sleeveless T-shirt – the royal blue of Everton, of course – and grey camouflage shorts, as she absorbed the buzz of conversation around her.

'Victoria was chatting away, she was lovely,' said Coleen, 'but I mostly hung out with Steven Gerrard, Jamie Carragher and Michael Owen and their girlfriends, because we're all from Liverpool.'

Alone at night, she snuggled up with Wayne to watch *Only Fools and Horses* on a DVD player, dissecting the day before joining their newfound celebrity friends at dinner. It was the stuff that dreams are made of: the dreams of little boys and girls who weave feverish fantasies as they fall into a slumber, knowing that, in all probability, they'll never come true. But it seemed as though starlight had fallen on Rooney: it had kissed him while he slept and fairies had plucked his dream for keeping.

The couple's love affair found breathing space on their first holiday alone, an eye-opening adventure in Miami, lazing on the beach and relaxing in the atmosphere of one of the USA's most celebrated playgrounds. It was there, during blissful sun-drenched days, that love blossomed from courtship to commitment. The prospect of a future marriage hung in the air and, just a week later, the couple joined both their families in the smart Mexican resort of Cancún.

'It was a dream holiday compared to those I went on when I was little,' said Wayne, 'but we were young and thought we might be bored on our own, so we invited our parents to Mexico. We had a villa and asked Coleen's dad if we could share a room. Coleen was nervous about asking her dad, but it was all right. I was a bit awkward at first, too. I didn't know what her dad was going to come out with, because he has a dry sense of humour.'

But while affairs of the heart were rapidly developing, the siren song of Rooney's first love was calling and, on 6

September 2003, he answered it with a passion that took the nation's breath away. Another record toppled, as Wayne became the youngest England player ever to score in a full international, netting the first goal in a 2–1 Euro 2004 qualifier against Macedonia.

Coleen, who had just returned to school to start her A-levels, had to be content with watching her hero shoot his way to victory on the TV at home.

'When the goal went in I couldn't believe it. I was rooted to the spot for a moment; I didn't think or do anything. Then, when it sank in, I jumped out of my chair and started screaming and cheering. My dad's a Liverpool supporter, but the whole family were leaping around and hugging each other. I was so proud of him.'

Rooney later admitted that he was just as gob-smacked and so blinded by euphoria that he didn't know what to do or where to run after he had scored.

He may have been just 17 years old but, with the same certainty that had propelled his football boots, he knew where his romantic heart lay and, just a month later, the soccer star formally proposed to his sweetheart – albeit on the forecourt of a BP garage!

'I had the ring made to my design. It's platinum and diamond – I know what she likes. Coleen had tried to interfere, but she made it too complicated. I'd picked it up from the jeweller and told her we were going out for a Chinese meal, but we stopped at a BP petrol garage to get money from the cashpoint. When she was getting the cash, I got the box out of my pocket and opened it. She got back into the car and I asked, "Will you marry me?" She was a bit emotional, she said yes and we had a bit of a hug.

Asking Coleen to marry me was worse than walking out for England.

'We didn't bother going for that meal. We rang Coleen's mum and told her to get the dinner on and went back to watch *EastEnders*. Coleen couldn't wait to get back and show everybody her ring. She loves it. When we got there, her mum had put candles on the table. It was really special.

'We'd already discussed getting married a few months earlier. We knew we were only young, but Coleen talked to her mum and she was happy for us. So were my parents when we spoke to them, but I was determined to ask her dad properly.

'I'll never forget the night. We were all sat in the living room watching TV and her dad already knew what was on my mind because her mum had told him. Eventually, after four hours of awkward silence, he finally said, "Haven't you got something to say to me, Wayne?"

'I said, "Can I marry your daughter please?" Then he gave me a big lecture and said, "If you love each other, I give my blessing."

'Then he told me to look after her, but said it was two people from the same area who loved each other and he knew it was right. Finally he shook my hand and her mum started crying.'

Even better, just a few weeks earlier, Wayne had passed his driving test – at his third attempt – and the couple could now seek the privacy they craved away from the bright lights of Liverpool.

Just a few weeks later, Wayne moved in with Coleen's parents after buying his own mum and dad a £470,000 home in Liverpool's upmarket West Derby.

By November, the couple were enjoying the kind of high-profile celebrity lifestyle common among the footballing elite: canoodling in a VIP area at a Beyoncé Knowles concert and, later, Coleen waltzing down the catwalk in a red mini-dress, raising cash at a charity fashion show.

Wayne became godfather to Coleen's sister Rosie, who suffers from Rett syndrome, a neurological disorder that means she is slowly losing her ability to perform everyday tasks like eating and walking. 'I was dead chuffed to be asked. Rosie has stolen my heart. She's very poorly, but always laughing – Coleen reckons she is always flirting with me. Rosie can't crawl, so I lift her up and put her on the bed and lie next to her and sing her favourite nursery rhymes.'

Coleen signed up with Wayne's agent Paul Stretford, landed a small part in TV soap *Hollyoaks* and quit her A-level studies. 'I just felt doing A-levels then wasn't right for me. I was getting offered acting parts, but I couldn't take them because of my schoolwork. I'd like to go to drama school, maybe to university, but there's plenty of time to do that. At the moment, I'm just looking after our new home.'

That new home was a £1.3 million mansion in Formby, a 20-minute drive from the council estate that had spawned their love – but a lifetime away from their roots.

5

Wayne was not just an exceptionally rare talent. He possessed self-discipline and level-headedness that accelerated his march through the ranks in the Everton youth set-up. He looked after himself and was extremely athletic: he had once considered boxing as a career and he possessed a footballing brain that many players don't develop until many years later.

When he was only 14, he burst into Everton's Under-19 side and scored his first goal at 15 – the age when he received his England Under-17 call-up.

But the opportunity to stake his claim as not just a bright prospect, but as an Everton legend came when he had broken Tommy Lawton's 65-year-old club record by becoming the youngest scorer when he netted two against Wrexham in the Worthington Cup at the start of October.

A month later, with the whole world now in on the secret after the Arsenal goal, Rooney travelled over the Pennines to Elland Road, where Everton had failed to beat Leeds since the day Dave Hickson made his debut in September 1951.

Rooney came on with 15 minutes to spare and scored the only goal of the game, after beating two players. 'I am banging my head against a wall to explain how Wayne Rooney scored that goal,' said Lucas Radebe, who was still picking himself off the floor when the ball hit the back of the net. 'I thought I had him. I don't know how the ball went through.'

Wayne and his strike partner Kevin Campbell were mobbed by a mini pitch invasion of demented Evertonians chanting, 'Can we play you every 51 years?' and 'The Queen has seen us win!'

Wayne said he felt as if he was scoring as a real footballer and, as an Evertonian, it was the best thrill in the world. That same evening he was back out in the streets kicking a ball against the wall with a gang of his mates. Panic-stricken Evertonians phoned the club to express their concerns.

Shouldn't this genius be wrapped up in cotton wool? Manager Moyes just grinned when told of the fans' anxieties. Playing with a ball was fine, he said, but, if anybody saw him doing anything he shouldn't, they must send him home. It seems that the whole of the blue side of Merseyside had taken on the role of surrogate parents.

Everton travelled to St James' Park for the third round of the Worthington Cup. It was 3–3 after 120 minutes and the game went to penalties. David Unsworth's was saved, Dave Watson put his away, Rooney scored the third – despite missing two in training that morning – and Kevin Campbell finished the job. It was the first time that Everton had won a penalty shoot-out since they had beaten Borussia Münchengladbach at Goodison back in 1971.

(That, incidentally, proved to be disappointing in the end, as Everton went out in the next round, the quarter-finals against Panathanaikos, losing out to some questionable refereeing decisions in Greece.)

The Newcastle fans took Rooney to their heart. They compared him to their Geordie talisman Paul Gascoigne. One Newcastle fan said at the time, 'He'll never be as daft as Gazza – but he could be as good.' With hindsight, of course, he has eclipsed Gascoigne.

There were few milestones for Rooney still to pass at club level, though he did manage to record another 'first' on Boxing Day 2003 when he was sent off in the game against Birmingham City. Many thought that it had been a very harsh decision for a relatively straightforward tackle, but what impressed everyone was that the minute the referee produced the red card Rooney just walked without displaying a flicker of protest, although, of course, he would not always be so level-headed with referees. He had become the youngest player to be red-carded in Premiership history.

That, however, did not prevent Sven-Goran Eriksson from including the youngster in his next full international squad on 12 February, when Rooney became England's youngest-ever player.

In April, he made his first competitive start for England against Turkey at Sunderland's Stadium of Light in a Euro 2004 qualifier and everybody was waiting for him to score his first international goal and thus become England's youngest scorer. He was awarded the Man of the Match accolade, but didn't hit the back of the net.

But he was a delight that night, as anybody who

watched the game will confirm. He did what players so rarely do and ran at the defence. Not only was he running at them, but he was teasing them with an array of tricks that, at one stage, included what seemed to be an attempt to play 'keepy-uppy' in the middle of the pitch while powering past astonished Turkish defenders.

His performance defied logic. To have so much confidence in his first competitive game for his country was astonishing. It showed, not for the first time, that one of his greatest strengths is his self-belief and his ability to settle in on any stage, no matter how big; in fact, the bigger, the better.

Rooney had to wait until the following season – and five months – to finally snatch the youngest goalscorer record off his England colleague Michael Owen. He did it in the away game against FYR Macedonia in another Euro 2004 game in September: he was aged 17 years and 317 days.

Four days later, he struck for his country again in a home game against Liechtenstein and, before the end of the year, he had increased his international tally to three, by netting against Denmark in a friendly that England lost 3–2.

At international level, his career seemed to be bounding ahead, but, at club level, David Moyes, Rooney's first manager as a professional, was determined not to move him on too quickly, and Rooney spent some of his first senior season at Everton on the bench.

Moyes is a strict disciplinarian who had had an average career as a footballer but who has now carved out an outstanding reputation as a team boss, and Rooney had a lively relationship with him. Since Rooney changed clubs, the two men have maintained a good relationship, and, these days, before a fixture between the two clubs, you will invariably find them chatting with each other in a quiet corner of the stadium.

Moyes was often criticised for holding Rooney back. Instead of starting games, the prodigy often found himself on the bench and, even if he did start, he was often hauled off in the second half. Rooney demonstrated his frustration and anger at being substituted on more than one occasion.

Some believed that sending Rooney on at a later stage of the game, particularly when Everton might have been losing, added even more pressure on to his still-developing shoulders. It was as if he was being taken off the leash and told to get on there and win it for Everton. The player himself never felt the pressure though; he just wanted to play, and, if in the process he could help Everton to win a game, then that was a dream come true for a boy who still glowed with pride every time he walked down the tunnel at Goodison Park and heard the *Z Cars* theme music blaring out.

Moyes has always defended his strategy with Rooney and he markedly points out that Rooney is now rated as one of the best. Here was a young man of exceptional talent, who would have played five times a week if he could. And in charge of him was a young manager who was handed the enviable problem of nurturing the greatest English talent to emerge in the game for decades.

For months after Rooney burst on to the scene by scoring that goal against Arsenal in October 2002, the manager kept his counsel on his protégé. The lad was getting rave reviews at international level and that again was fuelling the calls, mostly in Liverpool, that Rooney should start every game. There were even some suggestions that the club manager wasn't overly pleased that his player had become a regular fixture in the international set-up.

Talking ahead of England's home game against Turkey in the European Championship qualifiers in May 2003 at Sunderland, Moyes dismissed these claims, saying, 'Everton will have a team that will be good enough to give Wayne Rooney the platform that a talent like his deserves. He is such a natural. Even at this age he has the ability to do most things asked of him. I've warned people not to expect too much too soon of him and that's been regarded as a criticism of Sven-Goran Eriksson for picking him. But I was absolutely delighted when he called up Wayne. There's no problem with me that he is in the spotlight.'

Rooney went on to play in that game and was rated as Man of the Match in England's winning performance. His club manager was full of praise, but he still had a fatherly word or two of caution.

He said, 'He is capable of these performances and they will become more regular as he gets stronger and fitter. That's what we have to aim for, but we have to be careful. Hopefully, he has loads and loads of games to come for Everton and loads more caps to come for England. And if we think that, he doesn't need to be pushed today.

'I have to do what is right for Everton and, more importantly, what is right for Wayne Rooney. If you look at Wayne's performances, he did better as a substitute than he did in the games he started. He made a big impact when he came on and, out of those he started, he was very good – excellent in a few of them. Remember, he was a boy who had just come out of school. He'd had no full-time training.'

Further public support for the 18-year-old came in December 2003. Moyes did not know then that Rooney was to leave the club by the early weeks of the following season as a legend. But, as that legend was continuing to build, the Premiership's youngest manager said, 'He is a young boy who is doing terrifically well. We are very pleased with him. He is a special talent who is only 18 and we are trying to nurture that talent and bring him on as much as we possibly can.'

By late 2003, Rooney had only scored one goal for Everton, away at Charlton, but, by the New Year, he had boosted his tally to four. By the end of the 2003/04 season, he was Everton's top scorer with nine goals and he scored his last goal in an Everton shirt on 13 April 2004, when he hit the net away at Leeds in the 13th minute to give Everton the lead.

Ironically, just after half-time, young James Milner scored the equaliser. Earlier in the season, Milner had snatched the record away from Rooney for the youngest-ever scorer in the Premiership.

Everton's season ended with a dispiriting away defeat at Manchester City, where they were beaten 5–1. It meant that they finished just one place above the relegation zone and one place below that day's conquerors.

Whether or not the fact that Everton had had such a dismal season had any effect on Rooney's future – one that would unfold dramatically in Portugal and throughout the summer in England – nobody can tell. But there would have been a lot of wailing and gnashing of teeth on Merseyside if anybody had realised that, as Wayne Rooney trooped off the pitch, he would never be seen in an Everton shirt again.

Less than three weeks later, he scored another two goals for his country against Iceland in a pre-Euro 2004 warm-up game. Just over a week later, Rooney lined up for the start of Euro 2004.

Many doubters had expressed the view that Rooney was too young and too inexperienced to lead the England attack with Michael Owen, but they clearly had little conception of Rooney's talent or his incredible will to win. To appreciate the boy's genius, you had to have been watching him closely for the past two years, in detail. You had to be talking to people in football and listen to those that had spent years trying to spot a talent like Rooney.

There were fears that he would be overawed, that the stage would be too big or that he would shrink in the company of his peers, but they proved unfounded, and Rooney dominated Euro 2004. With him, England were simply unstoppable. He was a goal machine, creating and scoring in equal measure – until he was cruelly cut down in the quarter-final against Portugal after a clash with Jorge Andrade, who clipped the England striker's heel, leaving him with that now famous broken fifth metatarsal.

Without him, a vacuum opened up at the heart of the England team that was ruthlessly exploited by the opposition. The Portuguese knew that without him they were taking the firing pin out of a Gatling gun.

One individual who repeatedly failed to appreciate Rooney's talent was former England captain Tony Adams. He poured scorn on Rooney's two goals against Iceland and didn't think that he could fit into the England team alongside Michael Owen.

Rooney won the penalty for England in the French game

and was easily England's best player, before being taken off late on. The French players were queuing up to tell their favourite journalists what a genius they had encountered in Rooney. But this was not Adams's view. He urged Eriksson to drop him for the next game against Switzerland. Rooney's response: he scored two goals and achieved instant world fame.

Amazingly, Adams expressed the view that Rooney should be dropped for the final group game against Croatia, reasoning that he was getting in the way of allowing Michael Owen to score. Rooney's response: he bagged another two and Michael Owen, who had not scored in the competition, spoke of how great it was to play alongside his Merseyside compatriot.

As every England fan knows, the quarter-final against hosts and eventual finalists Portugal in Lisbon was there for the taking, but Rooney's metatarsal injury prompted an England stagnation which, combined with some dubious refereeing, allowed Portugal to draw the game at 2–2 into extra time and at 3–3 into penalties. England lost 6–5 after Beckham and Vassell failed to convert their spot kicks.

Rooney recalled, 'It was mind-blowing. I was just in a daze afterwards – it was almost unreal, absolutely gutting. Losing on penalties is the worst feeling in the world. At the end of the night I was at the hotel, waiting for the rest of the team to come back, and was just devastated we were out of the competition.

'All the hard work, all the hopes, had ended. We genuinely believed we could go on to win the tournament if we had beaten Portugal. I am convinced we would have gone all the way, especially when you look at the teams who were knocked out – like France, Italy and Spain. So to lose like that was almost too much to take.'

Rooney had gone into the last-eight clash in Lisbon as the tournament's top scorer with four goals. Euro 2004, to that date, was unquestionably the peak of Rooney's career.

But to the despair of the Everton faithful, the next time the England hero put on a football shirt in competition it would be that of his new club, Manchester United.

6

Although Rooney was a fervent Evertonian, to the extent that he once went to a Liverpool trial as a schoolboy wearing a blue shirt, he is also ruthlessly ambitious. After weeks of speculation following his explosion on to the world stage at Euro 2004, Rooney resolved to take control of his own destiny.

Those who have grown up with him know that he was born with the maturity of a man in his mid-twenties and, when he sets his mind on something, like dating Coleen McLoughlin or just getting a new mountain bike, he usually gets it.

His agent, Paul Stretford, is very much a man of the same ilk. Having spotted the enormous potential in Rooney, he entered into a round of business battles and court cases to acquire him as his own.

One of the reasons why there was such an explosive response to the transfer across the whole of the city of Liverpool was because of the way that matters spiralled to a head in the last 48 hours of August 2004.

Wayne was able to keep his head down as the inevitable

speculation, claim and counter-claim filled the back pages. Because he had broken his metatarsal in the quarter-final game against Portugal in Lisbon, he was not training with Everton and was, therefore, not in the public eye. But, if he had been fit, he has said that he would have played for Everton, no matter what the reaction of the crowd had been in the midst of all the speculation: it was still his club until any decision had been made for him to go anywhere else.

Had Rooney been fit, then he would almost certainly have been expected to play in the bank holiday game against Manchester United which, with the transfer saga going at full revs, would have caused terrible ill will.

The deal that took the Scouser to Manchester was actually completed the next day, though it is thought that all the details had been tied up between the two clubs at the Monday lunchtime match.

As the transfer window at the start of the 2004/05 season was drawing to a close, Everton believed that they had done enough to persuade their protégé to stay with the club he adored. However, there were undoubtedly some faint hearts both in and around Goodison. For those who didn't have blue blood coursing through their veins like Everton chairman Bill Kenwright, Rooney was seen as a cash-cow. Everton were struggling with debt and the value of footballers can fluctuate notoriously, depending on their form and their physical fitness.

If Everton were to get relegated the following season, as everybody was predicting, then they would have been forced to sell their prime asset in a fire-sale. On the back of the worldwide impression he had made at Euro 2004, Rooney was at his premium worth right then.

Bill Kenwright, the businessman, was well aware of that, but, instead of bowing to those who believed that the time was right to sell, he turned the argument against them and declared that the price for Rooney was £100 million and not a penny less. Kenwright was being theatrically fanciful, but he realistically believed that Rooney was worth £50 million, and that Everton shouldn't even consider selling him for any less.

Manager David Moyes was firing the same sort of salvos when he repeatedly stated that Rooney could only go for a record figure.

'We don't want to lose Wayne,' he said defiantly. 'But if we do, the only way is at the top price and the value we want... Didier Drogba went to Chelsea for £24 million, so Wayne's price should be a lot more than that.'

Despite all this resistance, hearts were broken, from the boardroom at Goodison Park to supporters' clubs all over the world when, with 48 hours to go, Kenwright took a call on his mobile phone. The very distinctive voice of Wayne Rooney was on the other end. He was distressed.

Sobbing, Wayne told Kenwright, 'I'm sorry, Mr Chairman, I've got to go.'

In a fleeting moment, Wayne's future had been decided.

A few minutes later, David Moyes received a similar call from the emotional young man, stating the same message, 'I'm sorry, boss, I've got to go.'

Rooney couldn't even get out the words to tell either Kenwright or Moyes that he was destined for Manchester United.

A shattered Kenwright, who was devastated by the sharp turn of events, said, 'When I got the call, I knew that things were moving on and there was almost nothing I could do about it. Nothing... It was obvious what a tough decision it was for Wayne to say that he wanted to leave and, although it went against every grain of Blue in my body, I had to try and understand why he had made that decision... It was the worst summer of my life. No one felt more pain than I did about Wayne going.'

And in a deeply philosophical mood the day after the transfer was concluded, he added, 'Wayne is simply the best prospect I have ever seen in an Everton shirt. The lad said in his press conference after signing for Manchester United that the transfer was probably much delayed because of the tremendous efforts Everton made to keep him and he is absolutely right.

'David Moyes and I had many meetings, both together and separately, with Wayne's advisers, and on several occasions we both felt that we were pretty close to an agreement that would keep him at the club. However, literally days before the August transfer window closed, it became very clear from Wayne that he really did want to leave Everton and, unfortunately, by that stage, David and I found that we had no option but to let him go.'

A few days later, the chairman received a personal note from Rooney thanking him for all he had done for him at Everton and expressing his regret at moving on; he also stated that he felt he had to make the tough decision at that stage of his career.

Kenwright said, 'It didn't really surprise me, because that was the sort of lad he has always been. Nevertheless, considering everything that had gone on in such a short space of time, and all the hassle surrounding the transfer, it was nice to know he was still thinking about us.'

To this day, Kenwright still cannot bear to watch Rooney play in a Manchester United shirt.

But it was never certain until the last moment that Rooney would go to Manchester United, and, in fact, Newcastle United started the transfer scramble by putting in an opening bid of £23 million. It was also rumoured that Chelsea might swoop at the last minute to gazump any earlier bid, aided by the seemingly limitless finances of Russian billionaire Roman Abramovich.

Despite Newcastle opening the bidding, nobody ever really believed that Rooney was going to go to the North-East. He wanted to move to 'a higher level of football', and, while Newcastle at the time were a very big club, their Champions League record was unspectacular and they hadn't picked up any domestic silverware for 50 years.

The transfer saga had come less than 100 weeks after Wayne had exploded on to the soccer scene with that goal against Arsenal. But from the start of 2004, there had been a persistent buzz around football, and in Liverpool in particular, that Rooney was going to Manchester United.

As early as the day after the 2004 FA Cup final, in which Manchester United beat Millwall 3–0, the *Sunday People* had reported exclusively that a deal with Sir Alex Ferguson, United's manager, was about to be done.

There's no evidence that any deal was 'done' or that Rooney had even taken part in any discussions about his future at that stage, but there did seem to be a general belief that he was going to be transferred to a much bigger club in the summer, and it seemed there was little doubt that Manchester United were the favourites to add him to their squad. He had mixed with United players in the England squad in Portugal and he yearned to be part of an organisation that felt as big and as successful as the Mancunian superclub.

Also, with his family connections, and those of girlfriend Coleen McLoughlin, it is safe to say he didn't want to travel too far away from his Merseyside roots; far enough to avoid the animosity he knew was coming his way, but not so far that he couldn't keep in touch with the community in which he had grown up.

On Tuesday, 31 August 2004, the transfer was complete. Outraged fans started to bombard local radio stations. There were reports of crazy death threats to the footballer and his agent.

It was impossible for thousands of lifelong Evertonians to understand how Rooney could have gone. It was a mystery to many how a young lad who had achieved the impossible dream of moving from the terraces to the pitch could suddenly give up his Everton fairy-tale.

Rooney had once worn a T-shirt that proclaimed, 'Once a Blue, always a Blue.' He wore it under his royal-blue Everton strip and flashed it to the adoring crowd after scoring against Aston Villa in the final of the FA Youth Cup at Goodison Park.

So was Rooney a traitor? Or had he – as felt by the largely silent body of fans – simply done what anybody else would have done in his shoes? Derek Hatton, the former firebrand deputy leader of Liverpool City Council and a lifelong Everton fan, said, 'If you were his dad, what would you have told him to do?'

In truth, Wayne Rooney Sr had actually played no part at all in his son's transfer. He had simply been caught up in the maelstrom. 'I was keeping track of what was going on by reading what was in the papers.'

As we shared a pint in The Winslow, a diehard Everton fans' pub in the shadow of the main stand at Goodison Park, Wayne Sr had just watched Everton lose 2–1 to West Ham to perpetuate their poor start to the season. In contrast, his son had taken the honours once again as the Man of the Match in a 4–0 victory over Wigan that kept United hot on the heels of Chelsea in their quest for an amazing ninth Premiership trophy in 14 years.

It had brought into focus the enormous dilemma of the Rooney family, who still supported Everton, while the boy himself was creating a worldwide reputation in a Manchester United shirt.

Clearly, this was causing the father at the head of a true-blue Everton family a lot of heartache, and he was clearly torn between the normal loyalties a father has to his son and the club that had been supported by the whole of his family for all of their lives. He said he wanted to continue with his life supporting Everton Football Club with as little fuss as possible, while at the same time showing a proud and caring interest in his son's career – just as any father would.

Though the Rooney family had hoped that their lives would not change to any significant degree, it soon became impossible for them not to be affected by the worldwide interest being taken in their son.

Even before Rooney left Everton, they had been forced to move house because, as Wayne Sr said to one neighbour,

'How many times can you put up with somebody knocking on your door day and night?' And it wasn't just people knocking on the door: it was malcontents causing trouble and damage to the Rooney family home and their cars.

When his son first returned to Goodison Park in a red shirt after United had drawn Everton in the fifth round of the FA Cup, it became a nightmare for the Rooney family. By that time, Wayne Sr and his wife Jeanette were allowed the use of a box at Goodison Park. But even in the privacy of that enclosed environment, the parents did not feel that it was right to put themselves in a position that would test their dual loyalties.

They must have been asked a million times in the weeks leading up to the game, 'Who do you want to win?' They never answered the question, because they were in the ultimate no-win situation. They finally decided not to accept the offer of hospitality on the day of the game and, because of their unique circumstances, have never commented on the outcome of it.

Their decision not to go to the game turned out to be a wise one, because more than one fan was spotted in the ground wearing a shirt bearing the slogan, 'We hate him so much because we loved him so much.' What father would want to subject his wife to having to witness that sort of behaviour, knowing that the bile was aimed at their son?

Wayne Sr understood why so many people in the city were devastated by his lad's departure to their arch-rivals along the M62. And, naturally, he would have preferred his son to have spent a glorious career regenerating Everton and becoming a legend alongside the likes of Dixie Dean, Brian Labone and Alex Young in the history of the club that was founded in 1878. But, nevertheless, he felt the strain of the continuing debate about whether Wayne was justified in pursuing his ambition or whether he abandoned the club he clearly adored when they badly needed him.

Part of the community in which he is immersed, and in which he has been all of his life, had turned against his boy. It only took a few hours after the transfer had officially been completed for the graffiti merchants to get to work on the walls of Goodison Park: 'Could Have Been a God – But Chose to be a Devil' was the mildest of the angry slogans daubed in white beneath the Everton crest.

Another read simply: 'Rooney – Judas'. Across the road, on the walls of Gwladys Street Primary School was the less restrained 'Die Rooney Die', this time sprayed in black.

The anger behind those slogans was defused to some extent by the fact that, following Rooney's departure, Everton, who were one of the favourites for relegation without him, had their best ever season in the Premiership. They qualified for the Champions League, a feat so remarkable that David Moyes was voted Manager of the Year, even above Jose Mourinho, 'the special one', who had brought Chelsea their first title for 50 years. In addition, nearly £25 million eventually flowed into the empty Everton coffers and, within two years, they were 20th in the list of the world's richest football clubs.

But for some – including Bill Kenwright – the pain of Rooney's departure remained unbearable, despite the financial compensations.

It is hard to know what sort of response Wayne Rooney thought he would get from the Everton fans; he must have known that a section of the Goodison crowd would regard him as a traitor. But it was through the transfer saga that Rooney's true character emerged. He revealed a rod of steel down his backbone.

Initially, he was clearly distressed at having had to make the decision that would take him away from the club that had been the focus of his life. The genuine tears to chairman Kenwright and manager Moyes proved that to be the case. But rather rapidly, as the confirmation of the transfer deal became public, the mood around Goodison Park changed – and so did that of the young Rooney.

By the time Everton played West Bromwich Albion at home on Saturday, 28 August, only their third game of the new season, a profound sense of shock had set in across the blue half of Merseyside. The transfer deal was in active negotiation. Everton were holding out for £30–40 million, but United wanted a staged deal involving bonus payments for appearances and the possibility of players in exchange.

While all this was going on behind the scenes, the public face of the Rooney transfer began to take a very nasty turn. Banners had been hastily put together by fans who displayed them during the West Brom game with venomous slogans like 'Judas'. The graffiti artists had already started their work on the walls outside. It had become obvious that he was going to come in for a good deal of stick.

Rooney issued his first words on the subject when he said, 'I am absolutely gutted at what is happening and now it is clear it is time for me to leave Everton. All clubs sell players, even Manchester United and Chelsea.'

And in response to the way that a faction of the fans had turned against him, he added, 'I am distressed at some of

Forever Blue? Evertonian Rooney's sparkling eyes give no hint of the future as he collects the BBC Young Sports Personality of the Year award in 2002.

Wayne takes his football very seriously, but not to the exclusion of enjoying a good laugh, *(above)* during training ahead of an England international and *(right)* even on the subs' bench for Manchester United.

Wayne Rooney shakes the hand of Sven-Goran Eriksson, the former England manager who gave him his international debut at the tender age of only 17.

Above: Rooney strikes again! This time against Denmark in November 2003.

Right: After breaking his metatarsal at the quarter finals of Euro 2004, it was not until the autumn that he was able to resume his glittering England career. Here he storms into space against Wales, showing his considerable physical strength and composure.

Above: Wife Coleen – childhood sweetheart turned glamourpuss and beach bunny.

Below left: Wayne's set to be one of the highest earners in world football. Sponsorship from sports companies such as Nike earn him millions.

Below right: The world's greatest young footballer at the FIFPRO World XI Player Awards in September 2005 – a huge accolade for a 20-year-old.

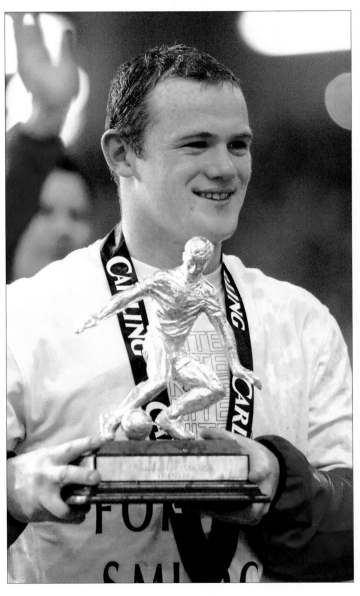

Man of the Match, Wayne proudly holds his award after helping his team win the Carling Cup in 2006 – his first senior prize.

Above: The deadly England strike partnership has worked before – here Rooney celebrates his goal against old rivals Argentina, with Owen in the background. Can it work again?

Below: Rooney at the end of the line for England, but still a key component in his nation's footballing dreams for a long time to come.

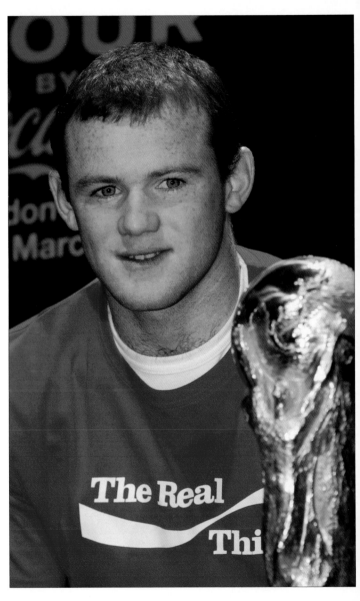

Wayne Rooney with the FIFA World Cup Trophy. Is this the closest Rooney will ever get to world football's most coveted prize?

the things that have been said about me, especially considering that I know the truth.'

And the truth was actually quite simple. A young footballer with clear world-class potential wanted to move on to what he perceived was a bigger stage and, while he knew that he was going to find it tough, he felt that he had no choice but to go ahead. He wanted to minimise the distress to his family, tens of thousands of fans and the club that was ingrained in his heart.

Rooney was at first saddened by the response from the fans and, in the months ahead, that sadness turned to anger as a faction of them continued to deride him. As far as he was concerned, it was a painful episode for a lot of people, but once the transfer was complete he thought that it was an issue that should be put to bed and that everybody should get on with their lives.

His inherent street toughness didn't always alert him to the sensitivities that people held over highly emotional issues, such as his transfer. When Rooney is wounded, he slaps mud on it to stop it bleeding and gets on with his life; in contrast, many of us Toffees are still feeling a painful rawness.

But his first words as a United player were conciliatory. He said, 'It has been a tough week for everybody concerned with me. It is difficult because I have supported Everton all my life and, having played for them as well for the last two years, it made it even more difficult. I obviously made it clear that I wanted to leave Everton and, once I knew that Manchester United were in for me, there was only one place that I was going to go.

'It is tough on Evertonians, because they always saw

me as one of their own. Everton are a massive club and if they had been in the Champions League it would have been a different matter. But I had to move on for my career and there is no better place to do that than here at Manchester United.

'After Euro 2004, I made up my mind that I wanted to play for a bigger club. The championships told me that I could play with top players in a big tournament and I wanted to start doing that week in week out … When you are sitting there and a lot of the England players are talking about the Champions League, you want to be a part of that. It is the biggest club tournament in the world.'

In his first visit back to Goodison Park after the transfer, fate had paired his past and present club together in the fifth round of the FA Cup. Tension built up in the days before the game: there were calls for increased security measures against protestors and even suggestions that Rooney might be stood down.

There was never the slightest chance of that happening. He made it clear that he was going to go into the lions' den with his head held high. He came out and warmed up at length before the kick-off and just ignored the abuse. United won.

At the start of Rooney's second season, Manchester United were due to play Everton in their opening game. This time he scored as United again won. Sometimes when footballers score against their old clubs, particularly on their home grounds, they shrug off the goal celebrations of their team-mates. Rooney celebrated in the way he celebrates any goal – arms waving, jumping and smiling.

More pointedly, when Manchester United equalised against Everton in the return fixture at Old Trafford later in the season, he took delight in the goal and made sure that the Everton fans knew it. His attitude towards Evertonians was now clearly, 'I will judge you as you judge me.'

7

Rooney's explosive introduction to his new fans is probably the greatest debut of the modern era. Bearing in mind that he had just come back from injury and that he was playing with a completely new set of team-mates, he could have been expected to ease himself in.

But that is not the way Rooney works. What happened was one of those 'were you there?' moments. It was simply stunning, as he slotted away a hat-trick against Turkish team Fenerbahce inside 54 minutes.

Throughout his first season, the teenager tantalised his new body of fans, his manager and his team-mates, not just with his skill but also with his incredible maturity.

His next landmark game came the following month against Arsenal.

Once again, the Gunners were on a long unbeaten run. In a tense and edgy confrontation, United gained the opportunity to break the stalemate with a penalty. The second-half award was full of controversy. Rooney was said to have dived over Sol Campbell's outstretched leg, but to others it looked as though he was merely anticipating being brought down and jumped out of the way.

Van Nistelrooy put the spot kick away and, minutes before the end, Rooney swept home a second to seal the three points.

It was a pivotal result. Arsenal, the reigning champions, were top at the time and United were only fifth, but it triggered a crisis of confidence for the Premiership holders and opened the door for Chelsea's first title in 50 years.

In November, Rooney scored two at St James' Park, the start of a remarkable record in a red shirt against Newcastle United in which he scored six goals in four league games.

The following January, he returned to Merseyside and antagonised the red half of Merseyside by scoring the only goal in United's victory. He even had a mobile phone thrown at him for his troubles.

In February, he produced an astonishing performance and steered his team to a 2–1 victory against Portsmouth with two of the best goals ever seen at Old Trafford. The first was a scoop-cum-chip over the goalkeeper from outside the area that would have done justice in its execution to a five-iron swing from Tiger Woods. His second was a volley that gave the keeper no chance.

His match-winning display lifted the club three days after they had lost at home to AC Milan in the Champions League, a result that precipitated their exit from the competition.

The previous week, he had made his first return to Goodison Park since leaving Everton. His new team beat his old one 2–0 in the fifth round of the FA Cup.

At the end of April, Rooney scored what has already

been billed as one of the greatest ever Manchester United goals. (The greatest ever is generally considered to be Ryan Giggs's solo run against Arsenal in the 1999 FA Cup semi-final replay, the year United won their Treble.)

It was an astonishing 30-yard volley and was one of those six goals against Newcastle United. The ball came over directly from a corner. Rooney appeared to be having a chat with the referee about a decision a few seconds earlier. Suddenly, he broke off the conversation as he saw the ball winging its way in from the left. He only took four paces before leaping into the air to smash the ball home, high in the net with his right foot. It was balletic and became a football talking point for weeks afterwards.

The last game of his first season was a terrible disappointment for the 19-year-old. Despite dominating old rivals Arsenal throughout the course of the FA Cup final at Cardiff, United ended up losing the game on penalties. The chance to pick up his first medal in his inaugural season had gone and, afterwards, he looked dejected and lost.

Reflecting on it he said, 'I hate losing – absolutely hate it. Sir Alex has instilled in me the importance of winning. You have to win all of the time. It doesn't matter what the game is, but obviously losing a Cup Final, especially when we thought we were the better team, is very hard.'

In his second season with United, Rooney found himself visiting his boyhood spiritual home, Goodison Park, on the opening day. He scored in a 2–0 victory and, perhaps to the surprise of many, he celebrated enthusiastically in front of the Everton fans. It appeared that he was sending out two signals. To one section of the Everton fans, 'You gave me a rough time,' and to the visiting United fans, 'Just in case you had any doubts, my heart now belongs to you.'

In the long term, United's challenge for the Premiership was once again eclipsed by the unstoppable force that Chelsea had become. And, by Christmas, the European campaign was over. Portugal was proving Rooney's unlucky country, as Benfica of Lisbon finished United off just as they were to dispose of Liverpool in the following round.

However, Rooney's single-minded approach to his football was never better illustrated than when he lined up against Arsenal at the end of the season.

United were still in with a shout of the title. Champions Chelsea were perceived at the time to be on the verge of a 'wobble' and were just seven points ahead of United at the top of the Premiership.

On the day, Chelsea were playing West Ham at home. On paper that was a fairly comfortable fixture and they were expected to win the Sunday-afternoon two o'clock kick-off.

United had the much tougher fixture, entertaining an in-form Arsenal at Old Trafford later in the day. It was vital that they took the three points, irrespective of Chelsea's result.

But the focal point of the day's events drifted away from the pure art of football as soon as the Sunday newspapers dropped on to millions of doormats all over the country. Rooney was alleged to have racked up gambling debts of £700,000, a figure later accepted by his personal management team. He had wagered huge sums on all forms of sporting results, except for matches in which he and his team were involved.

And it transpired that the money was owed to a man who was a close business associate of Michael Owen. Rooney's England striking partner had supposedly introduced his business manager Stephen Smith to his Merseyside pal who could deal with footballers' betting activities out of the public eye.

As soon as the story broke, there was speculation that the close bond between England's two top strikers had been fractured.

How then was this emerging saga going to affect Rooney as it unfolded hours before one of United's most important games of the season?

The pressure increased after Chelsea blew West Ham away 4–1. Not only did they comprehensively beat the east Londoners but they also overcame an early goal against them and a sending off that reduced them to ten men in the first half.

As the Chelsea game finished, the United match kicked off 200 miles to the north. It was vital that the Reds took all three points to keep up any hope of pipping Chelsea for the Premiership crown.

Any doubts about whether or not Rooney was distracted disappeared very early on. He was at his best, peppering the Arsenal goal with shots from every angle, drawing the very best out of keeper Jens Lehmann.

In the 43rd minute, an incident occurred which 12 months earlier could have sent Rooney into a lather. Ruud van Nistelrooy stroked a delightful ball into his strike partner's path on the edge of the area and to the left of the goal. Rooney hit it goalwards but it shaved the post.

At first, it looked as though he had simply misjudged the

angle but immediately he started protesting to the referee, indicating that somebody had handled the ball.

The problem was that his shot was so fierce and the ball travelled so rapidly that the human eye could not pick out what had happened. Several TV replays later from six different angles revealed that Arsenal defender Kolo Toure had dived across the flight of the ball and tipped it with his hands on to the post.

This was a dreadful infringement. United and Rooney had been denied a goal and possibly the advantage of having the Arsenal man sent off for handling in the area.

As the score was still 0–0 at the time and it was a few minutes from the break, which is the best psychological time for a team to score – and the worst to concede – it was a crucial moment.

It would have been understandable if the once volatile player had blown up at this significant injustice. And with that morning's newspaper headlines still fresh in everybody's mind, was the tinder-box about to ignite?

It didn't. In fact, after his initial and quite legitimate protest to referee Graham Poll, he accepted that nobody had seen it except himself.

It showed a new level of maturity in the boy. Nobody could really blame the officials. Even in a dozen TV replays, you had to look really hard to spot the handball.

But if Arsenal thought they had got away with it they were wrong. Early in the second half Mikael Silvestre floated over a made-to-measure cross which dipped over the head of Arsenal defender Senderos.

Rooney brought it down with an exquisite touch and before any other defender had a chance to react he lashed the ball into the net with a force that resembled a shell coming out of the barrel of a warship's big gun.

It was simply unstoppable.

Twenty minutes later, Rooney took Arsenal's full-back down the right wing and squared the ball for team-mate Ji Sung Park to fire home.

Rooney was voted Man of the Match and the odds on his being voted the PFA Player of the Year two weeks later shortened to make him favourite. Asked after the game if the gambling-debt headlines had been playing on his mind, he answered, 'I think my performance out there today answers that question.

'We knew Chelsea had won before we kicked off so that put extra pressure on us to get the result today. All we can do is to keep on winning.'

Later that day, Rooney let it be known that the gambling issue would have no effect on his friendship and his playing partnership with Michael Owen.

Later in the season, Manchester United's fierce rivals on Merseyside halted their FA Cup ambitions when they beat United 1–0 in the fifth round of the FA Cup at Anfield. That meant it was all down to the League Cup final against Wigan for that elusive medal.

As a club, Wigan had never been on such an elevated platform. In the event, United crushed them 4–0. Rooney got the first and the last.

He was easily the Man of the Match and, for the first time, he felt the elation of being a trophy winner.

8

At the time Rooney arrived at Old Trafford, United had begun to look a little threadbare. They were losing more and more components of the team that had given them a golden era from the start of the Premiership in 1992 until their last title in 2003. They also won the FA Cup in 2004, but lost out on the Premiership to arch-rivals Arsenal. And now Chelsea, powered by the pocket of owner Roman Abramovich and steered by the guile of manager Jose Mourinho, were a new force to be reckoned with.

Although nobody was going to admit it when he went to Old Trafford, he arrived with the huge expectation of the management and the fans that he was going to revive a United team that had suddenly lost its clear focus on where the trophies were and how to make sure that they gobbled them up.

One major concern for Sir Alex Ferguson was that his team had not become a European threat season after season, as Real Madrid had been in the previous decade and arch-rivals Liverpool had been in the 1970s and '80s.

A knife would be twisted into that particular wound when Liverpool, against everybody's expectations other than those of their own fans, won the top European trophy again in 2005 in the most dramatic final ever seen, coming back from a 3–0 half-time deficit to beat AC Milan after extra time and penalties. It took their total of triumphs in the competition to five against Manchester United's two.

Things had not gone smoothly at Old Trafford since David Beckham had left the club – ironically, for Real Madrid – after helping United to another Premier League title in 2003. Striker Ruud van Nistelrooy, no longer enjoying the supply that Beckham had provided, struggled for the goals that had graced his earlier years at the club. Beckham's replacement, a young Portuguese winger by the name of Cristiano Ronaldo, was showing tremendous skill and energy on the ball, but his crossing lacked the devilish accuracy of Beckham's, and he was being harshly branded a 'show pony' by critics. Few commentators could see then just how influential Ronaldo would become for the Old Trafford side.

It was Rooney who appeared to have been handpicked to be the catalyst for a new age of glory. But it soon became clear that even a boy of his talents could not single-handedly put everything right in a team that was, to use that ghastly phrase, 'in transition'.

United were having problems in midfield. The power-pack of the team in its heyday had been David Beckham, Paul Scholes, Nicky Butt, Ryan Giggs and Roy Keane. Beckham and Butt had gone and Scholes and Giggs displayed their old genius only in flashes, struggling to hold down a regular place in the starting line-up.

So much rested on the shoulders of club captain Keane, and the frustration frequently showed in both the facial expression and physical actions of the fiery Irishman. Could the arrival of Rooney relieve some of the burden from his new skipper?

Right from the start, Ferguson seemed to be in awe of his new signing. He said later that he had been after him since he was 16 and that United had even offered £5 million in those days, before Rooney had hit football's radar screen.

On the day that Rooney turned up at Old Trafford and signed for Manchester United, Ferguson assumed a benevolent, fatherly smile, one that continues to light up his face whenever he talks about the player.

Managers at all levels of the game are usually loath to single out any one member of their squad for praise but Ferguson has no such qualms about Rooney – neither, for that matter, do his other coaches at Old Trafford and even his team-mates.

Ferguson had not the slightest hesitation in shelling out a world record fee for an 18-year-old. And Rooney repaid his faith with one of the greatest debuts ever witnessed in modern-day football. He scored the perfect hat-trick in the Champions League tie against Fenerbahce at Old Trafford, one with his left foot, one with his right and then an unbeatable free-kick.

Ferguson battled with himself to try to play the situation down, because he knew the dangers of young players receiving too much praise too early in their career. Nevertheless, it prompted the United boss to say, 'It's a great start for him. That's why we signed him. He's got great potential. I think he can only get stronger. The important thing for me as a coach is to allow the boy to develop naturally without too much public attention. I want him to be as ordinary as he can.'

Rooney nearly tasted glory in his first season with United when he lined up in the FA Cup final against old enemy Arsenal. United dominated the game against a highly defensive Arsenal, looking tired after their ultimately fruitless race with Chelsea for the Premiership title, and Rooney was Man of the Match, but somehow Arsenal's rearguard action held out for a 0–0 draw, and they went on to win on penalties.

It was a rare trophyless season for United, though for Rooney there was recognition for his outstanding performances in the shape of the PFA Young Player of the Year Award.

However, the rumblings of discontent began to emanate once more from the club's own captain, Roy Keane. Everybody knew that 2005/06 was probably going to be his last season, but the club hoped that he would see out the campaign while they made the necessary moves for a replacement.

Not only was Keane regarded as the heartbeat of the United team, the powerhouse around which everything spun, he was also regarded as Sir Alex Ferguson in disguise. So when the two men fell out before the start of Rooney's second season at the club, it had a greater effect than if it had been any other member of the squad.

Keane had a history of speaking out when he saw things he didn't like. At the 2002 World Cup, he had criticised the Irish training set-up and been so scathing of coach Mick

McCarthy that the manager had had no choice but to send him home. More recently, Keane had famously turned his invective on the corporate brigade at Old Trafford for showing more interest in their prawn sandwiches than getting behind the team.

Now he decided he didn't like the idea of a pre-season training camp abroad being open to wives and families. As far as he was concerned that was like taking your kids to work.

Three months into the season, after United had entered a lull, Keane, who was injured at the time, started to publicly dish out critical advice to the team. While in the past this sort of outspoken behaviour appeared to have had the 'blind-eye' blessing of boss Ferguson, these new attacks on team-mates were becoming too bitter to be acceptable.

Keane was acquiring a reputation of being too much of a loose cannon for his own good... and for that of the club. So concerned were the coaches they asked their own cable TV station, MUTV, to be vigilant when it next came to interviewing him.

When that interview took place, it was so explosive and critical that the MUTV producers decided to refer it back to the club and Ferguson. It was immediately canned, but the contents of the interview inevitably leaked out and caused a huge row. Shortly afterwards, the long-standing skipper and United parted 'by mutual consent'.

Around the same time, Paul Scholes, rated by many as the finest pure footballer in Britain, suffered a mysterious double-vision problem just as he was coming back into top form. Sir Alex was struggling with a lack of pace and persuasion in midfield, trying to plug the gap by moulding

Alan Smith, bought as an attacker, into the job. Even Rio Ferdinand was played as a holding midfield player when United walloped Wolves 3–0 in the FA Cup, after which hysterical headlines demanded that Rio should take up the same role for England in the World Cup.

It was no wonder then that, within this footballing kaleidoscope, it was difficult for United to determine Wayne Rooney's best position: it all seemed to depend on the strength of the other players available for each match.

It's a testament to Rooney's contribution that season, together with that of the increasingly brilliant Ronaldo, that United remained the main challengers to champions Chelsea, and pushed them all the way to that fateful match at Stamford Bridge, where Chelsea's title celebrations were muted by the sight of Wayne Rooney being stretchered off, having broken his fourth metatarsal.

Named PFA Young Player of the Year for the second year running – an honour achieved by Ryan Giggs and Robbie Fowler before him – he had become such a major player for club and country that the prospect of his absence had England fans giving up on the World Cup six weeks before it had even begun.

9

In two seasons at Manchester United, Wayne Rooney had nothing more to show for his efforts than a League Cup winners medal, gained in a 4–0 thrashing of Wigan Athletic in Cardiff, with goals from Ronaldo, Louis Saha and two from Rooney. But such had been his rise to prominence that such eminent observers as Franz Beckenbauer and George Best were stating that, if he could come out of the World Cup as a winner, he would be viewed as the best player on the planet.

As England looked forward to the World Cup and prayed that Rooney would regain fitness in time to play, he told the *News of the World*, 'The World Cup is the biggest tournament any of us will ever play in and we have a squad that can go all the way. The nation is behind us and we want to deliver. This is a golden generation for English football and we know we all have to step up to the plate if we are going to win. But we have the ability and we do not fear anyone.

'Brazil are probably the best team in the world at the moment. We know it will be tough if we do play them, but we will stand up, give our all and make sure we are better than them on the day. There is a feeling that we owe them one after the last World Cup in Japan. I have spoken to the lads and I know that those who were there are still hurting about it.

'Ronaldinho has said that we can get to the final and that would be a dream for me. To play against Brazil would be brilliant and to get to a World Cup final and then face the team acknowledged as the best in the world would be the greatest challenge ever. As long as we get to the final, I won't care who we play. Of course, I would love to score in the final, but I won't be bothered as long as we win.

'The fact that people expect so much of me is not a burden. I don't feel that it is a weight. In fact, I quite enjoy the sensation. Of course, it's a real buzz to be talked about alongside the likes of Ronaldinho, David Beckham and other big stars, but I try not to think about it. The European Championships were very good for me until we got knocked out by Portugal after I broke my foot. I was gutted. Now I want to carry on where I left off.

'It's a big advantage having the finals in Germany. I know how some of the lads struggled in the Far East and this is probably our best chance in a long time.'

Rooney had acknowledged the threat of the Brazilians, who had knocked England out in 2002 and were now, if anything, stronger. We were constantly reminded of the talents of Ronaldo – the Brazilian legend, not Rooney's United team-mate, although it would turn out to be the latter who would become England's nemesis – Robinho, Adriano and Ronaldinho. Here were four fine footballers with great individual skills, but, under close examination, they each lacked one or more of the characteristics that made Wayne Rooney a more complete player.

Ronaldo was on the downward slope of his career. As each month went by, you got the impression that he had to work harder and harder to keep on top of his fitness.

Adriano was a player who had not yet settled down to make his mark with any one club. At 23, he was already into his second spell at Inter Milan after a carousel ride around Italian football that took in Fiorentina and Parma. A kid from the slums of Rio de Janeiro, he had burst on to the scene as a 17-year-old with Flamengo. He seemed to be a better player at international level than for his various clubs, having scored 21 times for Brazil in 28 appearances. His big problem was that his best position seemed to be in the role occupied by Ronaldinho, the World Player of the Year.

Ronaldinho had been outstanding for Barcelona, and was probably the best purely attacking player in the world. But it doesn't matter how good he and the others were in their respective positions. What none of them could do was operate comfortably in more than one area of the pitch.

The Brazilian boy hoping to stake his claim as the new sensation at the World Cup was Robinho. Born Robson De Souza, he had emerged from a dusty Brazilian backstreet and started playing football on the beach with pieces of discarded fruit found in the gutters around his basic home. Anything would do – an orange or even a plum – as long as it was something that was vaguely round and that he could keep up in the air.

According to his mother, he was the easiest child to buy presents for. All he ever wanted out of the meagre family budget was a new football – or, if possible, a real pair of football boots.

He was inevitably compared to the original Brazilian legend Pelé, but this time by the man himself. 'He reminds me of me,' said Pelé. 'The first time I saw him I got goosebumps. I almost cried. His dribbling was just devastating, so was the simplicity with which he controlled the ball.'

Like Rooney, Robinho became the teenage sensation of his football-mad country. But he did not make a first-team debut until he was 18, two years behind his English counterpart. However, when it came, he stayed in the team and helped Santos to win their first domestic title in 21 years.

He is best remembered in Brazil for a mesmerising performance against Corinthians that gave Santos their title. Running at a hapless defender, Robinho stepped over the ball eight times before he was dragged down in the penalty area. Not to be outdone by the frustrated full-back, he stepped up and scored from the spot.

Rooney was first capped at 17 and, as a result, had played in and made a huge impact on Euro 2004. Robinho still had to make his presence felt at an international tournament. But, nevertheless, he had become the football icon of the southern hemisphere and, since moving to Real Madrid for £15 million, had begun to light up the stadiums of Spain and Europe, albeit in a mediocre season for the club – further echoes of Rooney's own career.

But, while many people assumed Brazil would be the big threat, there were serious question marks over the team as a whole. Rooney, on the other hand, would be a key component in a far better constructed unit.

With his miraculous performance in the 2005 Champions League final, Steven Gerrard had staked a claim to be the best midfield player in the world, and one of the few players who could challenge him for that title was his England team-mate Frank Lampard.

John Terry, Lampard's Chelsea clubmate, had just lifted a second consecutive Premiership trophy and was being hailed as one of the best centre-backs in the world, as well as a vocal and motivational captain. With Rooney's clubmate Rio Ferdinand alongside him, and Ashley Cole – on the brink of joining Chelsea from Arsenal – excelling as a raiding full-back in the Roberto Carlos mould, England's defence looked far more solid than Brazil's.

'England have a lot of players who can help us win the World Cup,' said Rooney. 'Our squad is very good now – it's even better than the one from 2004.

'My main target has to be winning the Premiership with United. As a kid, that is the competition that I always dreamed of. World Cups were too far away in those days to dream about. But winning the World Cup – that would be pretty good, too.'

As it turned out, neither Brazil nor England stamped their authority on the 2006 World Cup. Rooney's injury kept him out of the first two group matches, and just prior to the tournament there had been a row between the England manager and Manchester United over the expectations being placed on his recovery. United had been through the very same situation four years earlier with David Beckham, and Ferguson felt there was no way Rooney would be fit until the knock-out stages; Eriksson begged to differ.

Even Sir Bobby Charlton was drawn into the argument, wearing his United director's hat. 'If we take a chance on putting Wayne in too early, it's not right for him. That's not being selfish for Manchester United; it's about being realistic for the lad himself.'

But Eriksson hit back in determined fashion. 'The good news is Wayne Rooney has no more injury. He is injury-free. Now it's up to us to get him match fit and, when we think he is match fit, I'm prepared to take in any specialist we want to take in or Manchester United want to take in.

'Professor Angus Wallace [the UK's leading metatarsal specialist] this morning assured me that he will be here when we think he is match fit. I'm prepared to listen to everyone and discuss with them about Rooney, but the last say in this story is Rooney's and mine.

'I am doing this in the best interest of Rooney, the England team and 40 million England fans. I'm responsible for it. I don't want any more discussions about Rooney until I tell you I think he is match fit. I don't want my players talking about Rooney's foot.'

In the end, Rooney returned, much to the delight of every England fan, for the 2–2 draw with Sweden, partnering first Michael Owen, then Peter Crouch up front, as England qualified top of the group.

In the next game, however, Sven-Goran Eriksson reverted to playing Rooney as a lone striker, a role he applied himself to willingly, though it was to prove a lonely and frustrating experience. A goal from Beckham was enough to send England through, and in the quarter-final they faced Portugal.

Again Rooney played alone up front, where he fought

manfully, often outnumbered four to one. The Portuguese players could sense his frustration and knew that it wouldn't take too much to ignite his notoriously short fuse. Cristiano Ronaldo, his United team-mate, was seen trying to wind him up before the start of the second half, and, when some persistent fouling by two Portuguese defenders, unpunished by referee Horacio Elizondo, provoked Rooney to stamp on Chelsea's Ricardo Carvalho, Ronaldo was first in beseeching Elizondo to show the red card.

He duly obliged. Rooney was sent off in the 62nd minute, and Ronaldo's wink to his team-mates, captured on camera for the world to see, ensured he would be public enemy number one when he returned to Premier League action in August – if, indeed, he had the nerve to return to England at all.

To cap it all, Ronaldo scored the winning penalty as the game concluded in another depressing shoot-out, leaving England, and Rooney, to lick their wounds.

Now the question on everybody's lips was not 'Could Rooney become the best player in the world?' but 'How could he and Ronaldo continue to play together in the same United team?'

10

As the 2006/07 season kicked off, all eyes were on Old Trafford as United played hosts to Fulham. Throughout the summer, there had been speculation over Ronaldo's future in England. A move to Real Madrid had seemed inevitable. Ronaldo had made no secret that it had been his boyhood dream to play for the Spanish giants. And even the least hysterical commentators seemed to think there was no way he could continue to ply his trade in England, least of all alongside Wayne Rooney, after his antics at the World Cup.

But Sir Alex Ferguson was more pragmatic. Ronaldo, like Rooney, had grown to be one of the best players in the world. Why should he dispense with him over something he had done against England?

Indeed, Ferguson had been through a very similar situation with David Beckham, after the player had been sent off against Argentina in 1998 and become the object of venomous public rebuke. On this occasion, Rooney was the first to try to patch things up, as Ferguson later revealed.

'Wayne phoned me on the day of the World Cup final and said he had a great idea. He suggested he could do a TV interview with Ronaldo and they could show everything was fine. I thought it would look stage-managed and said no.

'Instead, David Gill [United's chief executive] and I flew to Portugal to meet Ronaldo. We told him we'd had a similar experience with David Beckham. Ronaldo was concerned but not afraid [about coming back]. We said we'd put extra security on his house. He said he'd try it and see how it went. It's been no bother.'

Sure enough, when the team sheets were handed in on 20 August, there was Ronaldo in the same starting XI as Rooney. And it took all of 19 minutes to allay any concerns over the pair's willingness to play together.

By that time, United were 4–0 up, and both Rooney and Ronaldo were on the score-sheet. Rooney added his second after 64 minutes and the game ended 5–1 to United.

Three more victories followed in the league before a 1–0 defeat at Arsenal brought the run to an end. But United regained top spot on 1 October with a 2–0 win over Newcastle, and remained there until the end of the season. Wayne Rooney had achieved his boyhood dream of winning the Premiership.

'For my first couple of years at United, Chelsea looked so strong. They looked impossible to beat and I was thinking, But I came here to win things and I'm not winning anything. And then we knew that we, the players, really had to buck ourselves up to challenge them.'

And so they did. Indeed, right up until May, another Treble had looked more than possible. United, in scintillating form, had stormed through to the semi-finals of the Champions League with a 7–1 home win over Roma (8–3 on aggregate) and had booked their place in the FA Cup final where they would face Chelsea. Rooney and Ronaldo had been among the goalscorers, netting a total of 23 each for the season. They had become inseparable.

Defeat to AC Milan in the Champions League semi-final and a tired 1–0 loss at Wembley meant they had to be happy with the Premiership alone, but something had begun at Old Trafford. Fergie had done it again. Having been written off, told he should have retired when he first planned to three years earlier, he had built yet another championship-winning Manchester United side. And Wayne Rooney's decision to move to the club in search of the big prizes had been vindicated.

The knives were out again, however, when United began the following season with two draws and a defeat. Held 0–0 by Reading at Old Trafford in their opening game, they then drew 1–1 with Portsmouth, playing with ten men after Ronaldo was dismissed for an apparent headbutt.

Next up: Manchester City. And a 1–0 win for the blue side of Manchester sounded alarm bells at Old Trafford. You didn't have to look far for the root cause of the problem: no Rooney or Ronaldo.

Rooney had broken yet another metatarsal, this time in his left foot, against Reading and would be out for six weeks. And Ronaldo was serving a suspension for his red card against Portsmouth. But the pair were back together on goal-scoring form on 6 October in a 4–0 win over Wigan that sent United to the top of the table.

Four days earlier, Rooney had made his first appearance

since the injury and scored United's winner in a Champions League group match against Roma at Old Trafford. The team was beginning to purr. They had followed the City defeat with eight straight wins, including a 2–0 home win over Chelsea, managed for the first time by Avram Grant, after the sacking of Jose Mourinho.

But Chelsea remained a force, as did Arsenal, and Liverpool were getting stronger, too. This was not going to be a procession to the title. United sat in second place for most of the season up to Christmas, just on the shoulder of the leaders like a good distance runner. Then, with timing that had become a hallmark of Fergie's United sides, they cruised to the front on 12 January with a 6–0 thrashing of Newcastle United that included a hat-trick for Ronaldo and two from Argentinean Carlos Tevez, who had been added to the strikeforce from West Ham at the start of the season.

Rooney had missed more games in November with an ankle injury, including a crucial Euro 2008 qualifier against Croatia at Wembley. He could only watch in dismay as Steve McClaren's England dissolved in the rain, missing out on qualification and spelling the end of McClaren's reign.

But throughout Rooney's career, one door closing has meant another one opening, and in McClaren's place came Fabio Capello, the Italian with the tough exterior, who would knock England back into shape for the 2010 World Cup.

March is historically the time when United hit top gear, and so it was again. Having regained top spot on 15 March with a 1–0 win at Derby, courtesy of Ronaldo, they held on to clinch a second successive title on the last day of the season.

Ronaldo had scored an incredible 31 league goals, 42 in total, but it had not been plain sailing. Chelsea had pushed them all the way, and now, having lost out in the Premier League, the Londoners had a chance for revenge in the Champions League.

Both teams had won through to the final, to be held in Moscow, stronghold of Chelsea owner Abramovich, on 21 May. For Rooney, it was yet another milestone in his determined ascent to the pinnacle of world football.

'Chelsea are a big, physical team and they have players who can win the game for them from nothing. We know it's going to be a difficult game,' said Rooney.

He then paid a compliment to the man he had tangled with at the World Cup two years earlier. 'I would say Carvalho is probably the hardest defender I've ever played against. He's strong, quick and reads the game very well. John Terry's a big, strong defender and he'll never give in. They complement each other well.'

United dominated the first half and took the lead after 26 minutes with a Ronaldo header. But when Chelsea equalised just before half-time with a slightly fortuitous goal from Frank Lampard, the momentum swung in favour of the Londoners.

United lost their rhythm in the second half and the game went into extra time, in which neither team managed to forge the crucial opening. And so to penalties.

Rooney was spared the pressure, having been substituted for Nani in extra time, but, when Ronaldo stepped up and missed, it felt like it wasn't going to be

United's night. With the scores standing at four pens each and Chelsea with one in hand, John Terry stepped up to apply the coup de grace.

Amazingly, he missed.

The drama went to sudden death. Anderson scored for United, followed by Kalou, then Giggs... But Nicolas Anelka failed to convert his spot kick, and the glory was United's. Now Wayne Rooney had his own tale to tell of thrilling Champions League finals in exotic foreign fields.

It was the start of a memorable summer for Wayne and Coleen. They had planned to get married in June, and the triumph in Moscow just added to the feel-good factor as they headed off to Santa Margherita Ligure on the Italian Riviera for the wedding.

Only a few family members attended the wedding ceremony, plus the ubiquitous *OK!* magazine, which had agreed a reputed £2.5 million deal for exclusive coverage of the nuptials. Coleen wore a white dress and pearls, while Wayne wore a hazel-coloured suit with an open-necked shirt.

They were then whisked away in blacked-out limos to the nearby abbey at La Cervara, where the lavish reception took place and Wayne grabbed the mic to croon along with Westlife.

A year later, and he'd be back in Italy for another major extravaganza: a second consecutive Champions League final, this time against Barcelona in Rome. But, having begun brightly, United fell behind and immediately appeared to lose all confidence. From then on the result was never in doubt and the Spanish side dazzled, with mesmerising performances from its creative wizards Xavi,

Iniesta and Messi. The match ended 2–0 to Barcelona, marking a disappointing end to an otherwise magnificent season for United. It also marked the end of Ronaldo's career at Old Trafford.

For a couple of years, there had been rumour and speculation about his moving to Real Madrid, and when it was finally confirmed it came as no surprise. United could have no complaints. He had helped them to three consecutive titles, scoring a total of 91 goals in those three seasons, together with the Champions League and two League Cups, the latest having come that March against Spurs.

Once again, United had taken the Premiership by storm in the second half of the season, hitting top spot for the first time on 17 January and staying there for the remainder of the season. And, once again, Rooney and Ronaldo had been the stars of the show, with 12 and 18 league goals respectively.

Rooney says, 'The first league title I won, we dominated from day one until the end of the season, and from then on we've gone on and won the Champions League and two more titles. It's been an amazing three years.'

But with Ronaldo gone, what would happen in 2009/10?

11

The departure of Cristiano Ronaldo raised many questions over the future of Manchester United. Did they have the quality to make up for his loss? Who could they buy with the record £80 million transfer fee that could possibly fill his boots? And with Carlos Tevez being allowed to go to Manchester City, wasn't there a bit too much resting on the admittedly broad shoulders of Wayne Rooney to score the goals?

One question that was dealt with once and for all, however, was where exactly should Rooney play? A feature of his career to date had been his versatility and willingness to play wherever required. He had put in some brilliant performances playing on the left. He was also a shrewd operator playing behind a big striker. And, of course, he could lead the line.

Questioned on the subject, Ferguson was unequivocal. 'Wayne is a totally different type of player to Ronaldo. I don't think the responsibility of getting more goals will affect Wayne at all. He's got the mental strength. He's proved that time and time again.

He affirmed, 'He will be used as a central striker this season. He goes on these bursts of goals, but if he can do that more consistently over the season he will get to 25 and above.'

Ferguson challenged Rooney to emulate Ronaldo by going on to win the FIFA World Player of the Year award, which Ronaldo had picked up while still with United at the beginning of the year.

'That's the challenge there now for every player,' he said. 'There are some great players out there. Kaka, Ronaldo and Messi are the best three at the moment and I think Wayne can get to that level if he keeps making progress.

'He is blessed with certain ingredients only certain great players have. He has that hunger and determination. They want to win every match, every training session. He is blessed with that and that will never change.

'You sometimes wonder about the criticism of the money players get paid. But then you look at the amount of effort Wayne puts into his work and he is worth every penny.'

Ferguson cast his mind back to when Rooney first came to the club. 'It was a marvellous start to score a hat-trick on his debut. It was a remarkable feat. But since then his progress has never disappointed us. When we signed him as a kid, we thought he would become a really top player and he is going in that direction.'

With Ronaldo gone, the need to get the most from Rooney's scoring instincts saw him assume the lead role at Old Trafford as the spearhead of United's attack. And how he responded.

On 4 November 2008, he had become the youngest player in Premier League history to chalk up 200 appearances, prompting a fresh round of plaudits for the young player, though his manager felt the best was still to come.

'You just hope – as with all young players – that when they get to their mid-twenties they are going to be the full article in terms of their authority and timing and decision-making and how they live their lives,' said Ferguson. 'These are all important issues when players grow up.'

On 22 August 2009, in United's third game of the season, Rooney passed another milestone. His two goals in a 5–0 rout of Wigan Athletic made him the 20th United player in history to score over 100 goals for the club.

He scored in each of the next three games, and by the end of January he had already reached the 20-goals mark, including four against Hull City on 23 January, the last three coming in a devastating ten-minute spell at the end of the game.

The following Wednesday, he was grabbing the headlines again, with a last-minute headed winner against rivals City in the second leg of the League Cup semi-final. It was a just reward for a brilliant performance by Rooney in both legs, and Ferguson hailed his striker.

'It was much better than Saturday,' he said, referring to Rooney's single-handed demolition of Hull City. 'I know he scored four goals but tonight his control in leading the line and his link-up play was fantastic. Overall it was a wonderful performance – world class.'

Rooney had been world class all season. With the defensive pair of Rio Ferdinand and Nemanja Vidic – widely regarded as the best centre-back partnership in world football – missing much of the season through injury, United had stuttered through the season, sometimes having to field the likes of Darren Fletcher and Michael Carrick in unfamiliar defensive positions in an attempt to patch the holes left by the commanding centre-backs – not to mention Wes Brown, Jonny Evans, Gary Neville and John O'Shea, who also suffered their share of injuries.

Given this roll call of injured stars, it was remarkable that United had managed to remain in contention for the Premiership title at all. That they had was in no small part down to the performances of Rooney.

But the striker rebutted any claims that United, still trying to fill the void left in their attack by the departure of Ronaldo, were entirely dependent on him. 'I don't look on us as a one-man team or see it as a great burden on me, it's nonsense,' he said. 'If I don't get the service, I can't score. If I don't, I expect others to, and we've done that well.

'We've shared the goals out well and it's certainly not just about me. We expect to win as a team, not as individuals.'

In truth, Rooney had been ably assisted by two of the old guard, who had been deemed to be on the wane when he'd first arrived at the club. Paul Scholes and Ryan Giggs had rediscovered the sort of consistent form that had made them stars of United's all-conquering teams of the nineties and into the new millennium.

Giggs, in particular, was playing brilliantly, as was recognised when he became the very popular winner of the BBC Sports Personality of the Year award at the end of 2009. And his rejuvenation had been kindled by the inspirational presence of Rooney.

He said, 'Wayne has taken his game to another level. Everyone knows what Wayne is like. He wants to be involved. He wants to set up the play and finish the moves. Sometimes you cannot do that but he has learned to be patient.

'He has developed his game so that now he is a goalscorer as well as joining in with the overall play. I know if I am putting the ball in the box, with his movement and bravery, Wayne is going to get on the end of things. Wayne has worked hard at that part of his game and he has definitely improved.

'Even if he is not playing well, he still causes problems for the other team. That is a very rare quality. Even with players who are genuine match-winners, if they are not playing so well, normally you don't see them. But if Wayne is not having the best of games, which is not very often, he never gives up. He believes he is going to create chances. He believes he will get them and he believes he is going to score goals. More often than not, he does.'

'You've seen it for England and for us on the bigger stages. That is what all the top players do. The best thing is that Wayne is still developing. He is 24 now but he is only going to get better. His appetite is strong and he is a great player to have in your team.'

Such praise from a United legend can only have encouraged Rooney further. He had already gone on record saying how he looked up to Giggs, and for anyone who didn't believe there was such a thing as a one-club man any more, Giggs was living proof that there was.

'I have always said I would love to end my career at this club,' Rooney reiterated on MUTV. 'If I can get anywhere near what Ryan has done it would be an amazing achievement, because I regard him as the perfect role model.

'You must have great respect for the way his life is and the way he handles himself. The things he has done throughout his career and the things he has won are unbelievable. Everyone looks up to him and if I even get close to the number of games he has played I would be delighted.'

A major factor in Giggs's loyalty to United, and indeed that of Scholes and Gary Neville, was that they had only known one manager throughout their careers at the club. They may well retire before Ferguson does. Rooney, however, will still be playing after Fergie has finally passed the baton. And when a new broom sweeps in... who knows?

But, for now, he was playing a blinder, both in his football life and his family life. His best result of the season had come at Liverpool Women's Hospital on 2 November, when wife Coleen gave birth to a son, Kai Wayne Rooney. Wayne was present at the birth and quickly settled into the routine of fatherhood, as he revealed in an interview three months after the birth.

'Over the last year, my lifestyle's changed so much. I used to go to bed at one o'clock in the morning and now it's 10.30pm. It's been a big change.'

On the pitch, he had also made a major contribution to England's almost impeccable World Cup qualifying campaign, with nine goals.

England manager Fabio Capello said, 'Rooney has improved a lot during the past two years and this season he has been fantastic. He is scoring goals and he is good for the team. Rooney has been United's leader on the pitch. For me he has improved in every area and in one part of the pitch especially, close to goal. I have watched him this year and he is showing a new maturity.

'When I met him for the first time after a few games, I

spoke with him and asked why he didn't score more goals. Why? The answer was he was playing too far from goal and that needed to change. Now he is playing closer to goal and scoring. That is where he can be a dangerous player.'

It was fast approaching the fourth anniversary of that shocking injury at Stamford Bridge that had delayed his entry to the 2006 World Cup, and quite possibly hastened his, and England's, exit. If Rooney had been crucial to England's chances then, he was invaluable now.

As one of the most open and interesting Premiership seasons ever progressed through winter and into spring, the nation watched Rooney's performances thinking not what he could do for Manchester United, but what he could do for the nation. And the phrase 'wrap him in cotton wool' was heard up and down the land.

12

In the history of the beautiful game, only the legendary
Pelé comes anywhere close to emulating the achievements
of Wayne Rooney at such a young age. The boy from a
humble terraced house on one of Britain's most
downtrodden housing estates already sits at the peak of
footballing history.

By his 20th birthday, Rooney had already racked up 26
international appearances. Now, with more than double
that, he looks destined to challenge the 125 caps held by
legendary England goalkeeper Peter Shilton – which itself
may well fall to David Beckham in South Africa.

On the subject of goals, his ratio of just under a goal
every two games could see Rooney become England's most
prolific goalscorer, beating Bobby Charlton's total of 49
goals. One also has to bear in mind that, traditionally,
players tend to be hesitant in the goal-scoring charts early
in their careers and more prolific as they play more games.

Charlton himself said, 'Nothing would give me greater
pleasure than if Wayne Rooney broke my goal-scoring
record, and I pride it very much, but I think that he

potentially is looking like the one most likely to do it. Being from my own club, nothing would please me more.'

Rooney had a big start on the footballing knight, for Charlton hadn't won a single cap by the time he was 20. The Manchester United legend is only one of a list of England's great players, both past and present, who had not even been called into an international squad by the age that Rooney was heading towards 30 full caps. Among the others are David Beckham, Paul Gascoigne and Gary Lineker. And that is not a phenomenon solely restricted to these shores; some of the most famous players of all time – including Zinedine Zidane, Roberto Baggio and England's tormentor in the 1970 World Cup, Gerd Muller – hadn't won a cap or scored a goal at the age of 20.

Now 24, Rooney is the most iconic footballer we have had in this country since Paul Gascoigne, who was as much a product of the Geordie culture as Rooney is of the Scouse, and who was hailed as the genius of his age and the greatest talent this country had produced since the World Cup-winning days of the 1960s.

However, if you compare the records of the two sorcerers, it becomes clear that Rooney is light-years ahead of his North-Eastern counterpart: it is something that places the young Merseysider's achievements truly into perspective. Gascoigne had to wait until his 26th birthday before he reached the same stage that Rooney had achieved by the age of 20.

The coach who guided Rooney through his formative years, former Everton manager and star footballer Colin Harvey, has no doubts about how far Rooney can go. He said, 'He can become one of the greatest players English football has ever seen. It's a hell of a tall order, but he's got all the attributes. As well as his strength, he's got pace, he's good in the air and he's a tremendous athlete. He's two-footed and, although he is weaker on his left side, he will work on that.

'He was England's player of the tournament in 2004, but that didn't surprise me at all because I always knew what he could do. He could become as good as Maradona. Even better. I think he's the best talent since Maradona and I've always rated the Argentinean a better all-round performer than Pelé.'

Of course, Rooney's future achievements depend on his staying fit. He broke the metatarsal in his right foot during Euro 2004 when he had only just burst on to the international scene; then broke it again only weeks before the World Cup in Germany 2006; and again at the start of the 2007/08 season. He is in good company: England colleagues David Beckham, Steven Gerrard, Michael Owen and Gary Neville have all suffered the same injury.

Many believe that Rooney's injury cost England the tournament at Euro 2004; once he went off the field against Portugal in the quarter-finals, it was clear that England lost both their shape and the game. But apart from what could have been two more games in that competition, it did not cost Rooney in the long-term when it came to the international calendar.

His second break certainly affected his preparation for the 2006 World Cup, and it's possible that it had a bearing on his state of mind in that fateful game against Portugal. There's no doubt that his absence from the United team after he broke his left foot against Reading affected the team as a whole in the next two games, although they did rally before he returned six weeks later.

It is a sad fact that some players are naturally injury-prone and have to battle throughout their careers to try to find a consistent run of games without the interruption of a knock, a strain or a tear. But Rooney is generally considered to be an injury-free footballer, in the same resilient mould as Frank Lampard and John Terry. There are a few reasons for this: some physical and others more psychological.

The first one was described to me by a Premiership professional. 'When you are lined up in the tunnel and you look across at the other team, you try to avoid Rooney's eyes. He looks like he wants to kill you. He snorts like a bull with his chest heaving in and out and sometimes he turns his back and starts kicking the wall with his boots. You feel sorry for the wall. I've even seen him punching the wall.

'The effect of seeing his name written on the back of his shirt is also unsettling, because he's made such fools of so many defenders that you just fear from that moment on that you are going to have a dreadful day.

'Then, just before the ref leads us out, he starts shouting, really bellowing, at his team-mates, most of whom are much older than him. He clearly can't wait to get going. You get the feeling that if the ref delayed us for just another few seconds there would be an earthquake in that tunnel.'

Rooney is regarded, even among his peers, as a 'hard' footballer. That doesn't mean that he goes around clobbering people, but when players tackle him they have described it as like hitting a lamppost in a darkened street.

He has tremendous body strength. He comes from a family of boxers and, according to his boys' club coaches, could easily have become a fighter himself. This manifests itself in the phenomenon of players bouncing off him when they are challenging him for the ball.

Once professionals have become aware of the fact that Rooney seems to have a protective shield around him, they are reluctant to go in again because they fear that they will find themselves winded or flat on their face.

Another factor that usually keeps him injury-free is his dynamic speed and his ability to avoid, evade and jump free from potential aggressors. George Best had exactly the same talent to keep out of physical trouble.

It is astonishing that, in ten years of top-flight football, Best was hardly ever injured. And that was in the days when referees were nowhere near as protective of players as they are today: tackling from behind was allowed; players didn't have to wear shin-pads and, if you ever went to a game in which Best was playing, you would often hear the opposition coaches shouting, 'Break the bastard's legs!'

Referees have learned over the years to be particularly aware of 'roughhouse' tactics against better players, but nevertheless it is still a testament to the guile of the Merseysider that it is so difficult to clock him.

Paul Gascoigne is a tragic example of a player who lost a huge amount of his career through injury. Amazingly, Gazza was only ever available for selection for half of the games in which he could have played. This constituted a real waste of talent.

So far, Rooney has had successful spells at two great English clubs. Everton brought him into the game from the age of nine and it was in a blue shirt that he exploded on to both the Premiership and then the world stage. To many, he will remain an Evertonian forever.

But, as he has explained, circumstances conspired to take him away from Everton and on to Manchester United. He felt it was right at the time and he has since pledged his entire future to the world's biggest club.

It's clear that he thrives on the biggest stages and United is usually recognised as being the biggest club in the world. Rooney has gone on the record to say that he wants to spend his entire career with the club, and although that is a noble ambition, it is impossible to see what the future is going to bring.

At Portugal 2004, the then fledgling striker looked on in admiration at the records of the Manchester United players in the dressing room. Today, he has a record to match. He is set to become the most valuable footballer in the world. Look at what has happened to former players in that position – Cristiano Ronaldo anyone? Their currency is so high that they become immensely valuable to a club as a marketable asset. What club, for instance, would have let Maradona go at his peak? None, you would have thought, but he changed hands several times, even though he was the best player in the world. It's because of the way that football works these days. Money is the most potent force in the game.

And the player is only one element that benefits financially in a big transfer deal. Sometimes he is powerless to stop a transfer, because circumstances whirling above his head result in him moving on.

Rooney also has to keep himself fit off the field. He

lives in a world where he has been a millionaire since he was 18. For a lad from a humble home, that brings terrible temptations.

Among his generation, Rooney is not regarded as either a boozer or a club-lover. Unlike others who have fallen by the wayside, he has been in a stable relationship for all of his short, yet dynamic, professional life to date. But the pitfalls are everywhere.

There are two outstanding examples of professional footballers who torpedoed the latter parts of their careers through abuse off the field. The most spectacular case in point is that of George Best, who died in late 2005 after decades of heavy, and often riotous, boozing.

But Best was not what you would describe as a 'sad' character. By the time he gave up playing football at the highest level he was only 27, but he had won big honours in the game, including the European Cup.

The second example is that of Paul Gascoigne, a far more complicated character than Best. The former England player has a self-declared drink problem, and he has a highly compulsive nature that he battles to control. Despite his talent, he had a largely unspectacular career, and he was blighted by injuries, which were slow to heal.

Those who know Rooney are aware of his single-mindedness and his terrific strength of character. He doesn't tolerate hangers-on or those who want to bask in his reflected glory. In addition, he has a very solid relationship with wife Coleen. So he is unlikely to be drawn into a life of debauchery unless he wants to be. And there is no evidence of that so far.

In fact, his desire to be his own man has been obvious

from the very first time he was drafted into the senior England squad. One other young player appointed himself as Rooney's 'minder'. There was tremendous public interest in the then Everton player, but each time a TV camera homed in on him, the other player suddenly appeared trying to put a protective arm around him.

After two days of this, Rooney felt that he could stand on his own two feet without any problem. He thanked his team-mate for the concern, but decided that, if he was going to have to suffer being under the spotlight throughout his career, then he may as well get used to it. He'd handled himself OK on the streets of Croxteth for the past 17 years, so he had no fears.

Footballers can retire these days with endorsement contracts for the next 30 years and, when you look at how the world gets richer every day, it's not beyond the realms of possibility to consider the phenomenon of a billon-dollar footballer.

As the appeal of the game continues to grow around the world, with ever-expanding TV networks and communications, Rooney is fast becoming a global icon. He already has a host of contracts with drinks companies, electronic-games manufacturers, boot suppliers, clothing labels and even supermarkets. And if he becomes the best footballer in the world and wins World Cups, his potential future wealth is almost limitless.

Every young professional footballer obviously has a desire for the game. It is often their ticket to escape from an average upbringing. Success in the game can, by comparison, give them entry to a world of riches and fame. But if that is their only motivation it is not enough.

Rooney entered this world of wealth and privilege at a very young age. Is this a good thing or a bad thing?

On the plus side, he got there very early and it's the only life he has ever known as an adolescent, so he will be desperate not to let it go. The danger is that he may begin to take it all for granted and become bored with both his life and with football.

When a footballer loses his desire to play, everything else collapses. The problems in modern-day football usually come mid-career. If a player aged 25 wakes up one morning to find he has lost his automatic place, he has two choices: either fight to get back into the first team or roll over and count the dosh.

Few players have actually given the game up, but many have drifted into a different approach to their job with the cushion of wealth that is beyond the imagination of the vast majority of the population.

You can't define desire in a footballer or spot the moment when it starts to dissipate, but a manager and a player's team-mates can pick up on it as soon as it starts to happen. But one of the men who has shaped both his life and his career, Colin Harvey, believes that Rooney has the desire to be able to build a spectacular and long-lasting career.

'He has all the qualities to be a great, long-term England star. He's got all the attributes. Desire is at the top of them, alongside his ability. I know him and I know what he can do in the future.'

Rooney's current desire and the inferno that burns within him, which drives him to strive for success at the World Cup, is born out of his desperate need to win things.

When he was awarded the European Young Player of Europe award in 2005, he revealed, 'As far as I am aware, this is the first international trophy I have won. It's the only thing I have ever won since I was a kid. It's a nice feeling and I want a lot more of it.'

However, shortly afterwards, he experienced the pain of losing in the big arena and that was an experience he found so horrible that he never wants to go through it again.

Manchester United played Arsenal in the 2005 FA Cup final at the Millennium Stadium in Cardiff. United dominated the game and Rooney was arguably the Man of the Match, but his team lost on penalties.

Anybody who witnessed Rooney on the pitch after Arsenal had snatched the game could see that the hurt was distorting his face. Even though he could have comforted himself that he had years ahead of him to win trophies, it was no consolation.

As the Arsenal fans celebrated their victory over their fiercest rivals for the previous decade, Rooney stood in the middle of the boiling cauldron, hands on hips, with a look of total desolation on his face; a look that was slowly turning to a snarling, burning anger. Losing, as he described later, is the very worst feeling in the world.

Rooney has never had the slightest concern about the quality of the opposition or the surroundings in which he plays. In his first game for Manchester United – the European tie with Fenerbahce – he scored a hat-trick, even though he'd never worn his new club's shirt before and it was his European debut. He said at the time that it wasn't any sense of fear that was going to inhibit his play that night, but the danger of getting overexcited.

The manager had told him he was playing two days beforehand and he couldn't contain his joy. He found it hard to sleep or to concentrate on anything except the upcoming game.

Anybody who has seen Rooney at close quarters will realise that he is unconcerned by his surroundings; he could be on his school playing field in Croxteth or in the Nou Camp – his desire remains the same.

It is generally accepted that Rooney is outstanding in at least two positions. He is lethal as an out-and-out striker, but he is equally efficient playing off the main striker or in 'the hole' behind the front two.

In this role, he is more likely to be providing chances for his team-mates as well as looking for goal himself, but it means that others may be getting their name on the scoresheet through Rooney's 'assists' instead of the boy himself.

This does not seem to bother the England star. We already know he will play anywhere as long as he is playing and he genuinely enjoys the thrill of setting up a team-mate with a scintillating pass or a cross as well as hitting the back of the net himself.

In training, he often likes to play in goal when the lads are winding down and has often wound up his team-mates at Manchester United by telling them that he is the club's best keeper.

Despite his humour off the field, Rooney the footballer soon became renowned for his volatile temper: in his short career with Everton he was sent off once and booked 17 times. That's a disturbing figure for a boy who was still only 18 when he left the club, so it was obvious that his new club, Manchester United, had to keep an eye on him.

His most explosive display of anger took place in Real Madrid's Bernabeu Stadium in November 2004, when he was playing for England in a friendly against Spain.

For reasons that have never properly been explained, England's youngest player went on a one-man mission of fury against the Spanish after the hosts had taken the lead in the 10th minute.

Not for the only time, Rooney was upset with both himself and his team-mates for having conceded an early goal. And he made this clear two minutes after Spain had scored when he lost possession and felled Spanish defender Joaquin. The Greek referee would have been entirely justified in booking him, but let it go.

Twenty-five minutes later, he pushed Spain's goalkeeper, Casillas, into a safety fence as the pair chased a loose ball over the line, and received a yellow card. Two minutes later, he sent defender Marchena flying. All the evidence suggested that he should have been sent off for a second yellow card, but the referee, George Kasnaferis, only gave a free-kick.

The England bench realised how lucky England were to still have 11 men on the pitch and decided that Rooney, in that mood, had become a liability. They withdrew him just before half-time and brought on Alan Smith in his place.

But the angst did not end there. The England players that night were wearing black armbands as a tribute to former national captain and Liverpool legend Emlyn Hughes, who had passed away a few days before.

Without thinking, Rooney tore off his armband and threw it to the ground as he departed the arena. It was seen

as a terrible insult to the Kop great who had won every
honour in the game, as well as leading his country. He was
immediately rebuked by Sven-Goran Eriksson and he
quickly realised his mistake. As the players filed into the
dressing room at half-time, he apologised to them and to
the coaching staff.

He sat out the second half in his England blazer behind
the dugout and the following day apologised publicly for
the perceived insult to Emlyn Hughes. He said he had not
realised what he was doing.

His club manager, Sir Alex Ferguson, later accepted that
what Rooney had done was wrong, but reminded the
world that his player's explosive nature was part of the
reason why he was such a fearsome player.

Rooney continued to pick up the odd booking, but came
to the nation's attention again towards the end of the
2004/05 season when, while playing for United at Arsenal,
he went ballistic with referee Graham Poll.

Television footage clearly showed him mouthing
expletives, over and over again, and Poll came in for
tremendous criticism for not despatching the firebrand
from the field.

I met Mr Poll the following day when he came to be
interviewed at talkSPORT and he was adamant that, had
Rooney sworn at him, he would definitely have sent him
off. But, in fact, said Mr Poll, he may well have been seen
swearing by a TV camera, but Rooney did not insult the
match officials, including the ref.

Inevitably, Rooney did receive his marching orders in a
Manchester United shirt – and it couldn't have been for a
more unexpected reason.

United were playing at the Spanish club Villarreal in a group-stage match in the Champions League. Their campaign up to that point had not been sparkling and they needed the win. They were drawing 0–0 when the referee awarded United a free-kick. Frustrated by his team's inability to score, Rooney mouthed off to the ref and was booked. As a sarcastic gesture, Rooney applauded the match official. And he did not do it in a subtle fashion. He clapped his black-gloved hands together right under the referee's nose. The man in black was outraged and clearly took it as an insult to his authority, so he whipped out the yellow card again, quickly followed by the red, and Rooney was off.

It was a sorry campaign for United. They failed to pick up enough momentum in the group stage to move on to the knockout games and they were out of the top competition before Christmas.

This became a watershed for Rooney, who consciously decided that the time had come for him to get a grip of his temper. Within weeks, he was seen to be adopting a different attitude to the officials.

Instead of running at them at full pelt, he started to take a more measured approach. He would approach the referee and explain to him where he thought the ref had gone wrong, often with a physical demonstration of how he believed things had happened.

Instead of watching a young man losing control of himself with the veins in his neck bulging as if they were going to burst, we witnessed a more reflective individual who was trying to reason with the ref that an opponent had dived or that a clash with another player had been an accident.

Rooney's renaissance was evident in both legs of United's Carling Cup semi-final against Blackburn in January. Blackburn's enfant terrible was Robbie Savage, the loud-mouthed journeyman who had a reputation for winding up other players, particularly by feigning injury after the slightest contact with an opponent.

He was involved in an incident in each match which involved Rooney and which, a few months earlier, could have had serious consequences for England's talisman.

During the first match, Savage went down under a heavy tackle in a tight situation involving several players. Rooney fell on top of him. Savage made the mad decision to grab the former schoolboy boxer by the throat, at which point everybody who witnessed it thought that Rooney would retaliate immediately.

But he didn't. He pulled Savage's hands from his neck, got up and walked away. For some reason he got booked, but he even shrugged his shoulders at that.

In the return game, two weeks later, Savage was again at the centre of an incident. There had been bad blood between him and Rio Ferdinand throughout the first half. As the teams trooped off, Ferdinand allegedly clipped Savage about the head as he passed him to the tunnel.

Savage sprinted after him. It led to a stampede by many other players into the tunnel, but with the pull-out cover in that corner of the ground nobody could see what was going on except the ball-boys at the entrance, who were apparently imitating what they were seeing by shadow-boxing with each other.

However, it later emerged that Rooney was the peacemaker who broke up the mêlée. He grabbed Savage's arm and dragged him from the main tunnel into the passageway that leads to the dressing rooms, leaving the other players, and even the Blackburn manager, to get on with swapping insults and shouting and swearing at each other.

At the end of the game, Savage and Rooney left the field smiling and sharing a joke, although Rooney had the broader smile of the two, as United went through to the Carling Cup final.

Before the 2006 World Cup, former top-class referee Jeff Winter warned that mouthy and abusive players would be targeted at the World Cup, then and in the future. And he added that Rooney's profile was so high around the world that, should he play, he was bound to be the subject of intense scrutiny by the officials.

He said, 'At the beginning of every tournament, and particularly something as important as the World Cup, the referees are gathered and given directives on what FIFA expect of them. Discipline is always high on the agenda. In the past, there has been a clampdown on red and yellow cards and a flurry of red and yellow cards has followed. With the image of the game being so important at the moment, they will be told to come down heavy on dissent, on swearing and on charging at officials.

'I can imagine the referees meeting before the first game and discussing how they will issue red cards to players running at them, mouthing off and gesticulating. The referees will be sitting there with this image of a player effing and blinding and they will think of Rooney... His name will be very much to the fore in discussions. Remember, the common language of referees is English and they know all the unsavoury words.'

Winter proved to be right. Rooney's reputation surely preceded him when he was dismissed against Portugal. The referee should have given him more protection from the Portuguese fouling, but leaped in as soon as Rooney retaliated.

It was an unfortunate lapse in what had been a clear effort on the player's part to improve his self-discipline on the field of play. But he has continued to work at that aspect of his game and, but for the occasional fit of pique, such as punching a corner flag at Craven Cottage after being rather harshly sent off for a second bookable offence, it's fair to say that it would be grossly unjust if referees at the 2010 World Cup are still pinpointing Wayne Rooney in their pre-tournament briefings.

13

So what can we expect from Rooney in the future? It's not just that he can play in more than one position; he actually does play in at least two different positions, no matter where his manager asks him to start. There isn't another player who pulls on a pair of boots today who can make such an overall contribution to a game.

Colin Harvey, his youth coach at Everton, has always believed that he is an out-and-out striker. That was probably born out of the fact that Harvey, who made his own debut as a teenager in Milan's San Siro stadium, was in charge of him when he was a goal-scoring machine.

Rooney used to play in teams full of boys who were two or three years older than him, and he was still able to score record-breaking numbers of goals throughout his schoolboy years. But, as he got older, it became clear that his talents were so extensive that he was just as able playing behind a single forward or two forwards, because he has the vision to supply killer balls as well as create his own goals.

He seems as comfortable setting up chances for his

team-mates as he does in scoring himself. And he also looks just as pleased by 'assisting' as he does by finishing the job with his own feet.

He is also brilliant when he runs at defences from deep; he does not score many goals inside the six-yard box. He is much more likely to get himself on the end of a one-two that takes him into the area, having perhaps started the move on the halfway line.

Or, alternatively, he could be lashing the ball into the back of the net from way out. He needs very little back-lift to generate such power in his shot that, if one of his cannonballs is on target, it has become a lost cause for a goalkeeper.

Then, of course, there is his ability to fool goalkeepers with a lob, to pulverise them with a volley from 30 yards or to leave them stranded with a deftly struck free-kick.

And Rooney clearly doesn't believe that his responsibilities for either his club or his country end at just scoring or providing chances up front. What is amazing about the boy is that he likes tackling other players. When did you ever see Bobby Charlton or Gary Lineker – currently England's two highest-ever scorers – throwing themselves enthusiastically into a challenge?

George Best did it regularly. It is a mark of exceptional players that they want to be involved in every aspect of the game and Best was indisputably the greatest player that Britain has ever produced.

United's first game after Best's death was against West Ham. Rooney had said in tribute to Best that he hopes he is remembered in much the same way. He then produced another ten-out-of-ten performance, scoring a stunning goal as United came from behind to win 2–1.

Ferguson said, 'I hoped that somebody would produce moments that would reflect George Best properly... Wayne is only 20 and without question is the best young player that I have seen in my time. If he keeps developing and matures, goodness knows what he will become. He's a breath of fresh air to the game. He could have scored four or five today. He produced some great moments.'

Though few people had ever considered Rooney as a leader of men, probably because he was still so very young, Sir Alex saw qualities in the boy that he thought could make him a club captain of the future.

He said, 'I think we have a potential captain in Wayne Rooney. I think there are indications there that he has the mental toughness, respect and the winning mentality that Manchester United captains need.'

And indeed, when John Terry was stripped of the captaincy for his dalliance with the ex-girlfriend of England team-mate Wayne Bridge, Rooney was one of the favourites to take his place. Instead, Capello promoted Rio Ferdinand from vice-captain to captain, but, as everyone knows, any great football team will have more than one leader on the pitch – and Rooney is one of those.

The Manchester United manager is taken by his focus and desire. 'He's a product of being brought up just thinking about football. There are many examples of that – Roy Keane, Bryan Robson, Mark Hughes – who combine that great energy and passion to play football all the time. It doesn't matter the kind of game; you get the same desire and commitment every time.'

Nobody knows how long Rooney will stay at Manchester United. That depends on the individual views of both the player and the club and it is very rare these days for a footballer to spend nearly his whole career at one club. Rooney may have pledged himself to United for life, but so much can happen over the next few years. Should Ferguson retire and a new man come in with new ideas and principles, Rooney may decide his future lies elsewhere. His principal motivation for playing football is to win things.

'My ambitions in a Manchester United shirt are quite simple. A club this size should be winning trophies. At this club we want to win every tournament we are in. First of all we want the league, but of course the Champions League is massive for us as well. The number of trophies won here in the past is frightening – the current set of lads want to add to that great history.'

Rooney has already gone a long way towards emulating the United greats and adding to that astonishing haul of silverware in the Old Trafford trophy room. The only domestic trophy he has yet to win is the FA Cup.

It is on the international stage that his true greatness is yet to be affirmed. While comparisons to Pelé, Maradona, Zidane et al may well be justified, it is not until he has lifted the World Cup that he will be able to stand alongside such exalted company in the pantheon of all-time greats.

The world awaits.

Tony,

The Positivity Tribe
In the Locker Room

by Christopher J. Wirth & Fred Quartlebaum

To Your Success!

I Believe in you.

#WRBLOU